T0194175

Pereginus

LINDA BOERSTLER

authorHOUSE®

AuthorHouse™
1663 Liberty Drive
Bloomington, IN 47403
www.authorhouse.com
Phone: 1 (800) 839-8640

Published by AuthorHouse   03/11/2020

ISBN: 978-1-7283-4643-4 (sc)
ISBN: 978-1-7283-4642-7 (e)

Library of Congress Control Number: 2020902300

Print information available on the last page.

Scripture taken from The Holy Bible, King James Version. Public Domain

Scripture quotations marked NKJV are taken from the New King James Version. Copyright © 1982 by Thomas Nelson, Inc. Used by permission. All rights reserved.

This book is printed on acid-free paper.

Contents

Introduction

This book serves as a smattering of journal entries from a collection of over 140 volumes spanning 35 plus years. It contains a plethora of original poems, reflective narratives, scripture references, brief Bible studies and comments. It shows the development of the life of one believer works her way through the vagaries and uncertainties of life.

From a young age I was obsessed with books and writing. In grade school I would "make" books by folding notebook pages into quarters and stapling them together in "book" form. Within those books I would write poems, stories, pictures and so forth. For me that was great satisfaction gained from not only reading a book but also from feeling the shape and weight of it in my hands. Creating a book helped me to do something with all the words that were, forever clambering for notice in my overactive mind.

Writing for me is a validation of sorts. It is proof of my existence and my usefulness on the planet. It is an attempt to leave something behind that will provide a spark that will ignite a fire within the heart of the reader. Is signifies growth. These poems were birthed when I reflected on things that were significant in my life, or a series of moments designed to capture something that were tangible, alive, and real. As a result, some present raw emotions that were evoked in the process of living though and handling the many situations of life, those real or perceived. Now when I go back to a specific poem, I am transported to the timeframe in which it happened as if I was experiencing it for the first time.

It is my hope as a writer for the reader to reflect and to contemplate what is written. I want to encourage discussions, emotions, connection and the realization that every human being will suffer from setbacks, hardships, and desperation. I want to show that we can be grateful for the joys, accomplishments, love, and family as well as for the hard moments. I am hopeful that the reader will discover new insights regarding their walk with God and how that translates to their personal circumstances; such as life, work and relationships.

The title of this book PEREGINUS indicates several concepts. First, a definition from Merriam-Webster.com defines the word peregrine as being one who is prone to wandering. Etymology tells us that that word is Latin and French in origin. A similar word is *pilgrim*, which denotes that a pilgrim is one who wanders from place to place with a single purpose in mind. These could be such as: visiting one's historical roots and connection or seeking to follow in the footsteps of another. Another facet of that word refers to the classification of a powerful falcon, a predator, that can be found in places across the planet. This creation naturally wanders from place to place in search of prey and habitation.

Please note that each poem, with the accompanying scripture references, mini Bible studies, and a narration is best read as having its own meaning singularly and can be meditated upon with a complete understanding of the specific piece. These poems are from a lifetime of gathering and writing and were spawned from different attitudes and knowledge as the writer matured into an adult. It is not necessary to read the book from cover to cover, although it is fine if you do so, it is rather a compendium or an anthology of that growing process.

May you become peregrine as you read and meditate upon this book and let yourself soar beyond the limitations of earth and body to find the meaning of your individual journey and how that will define your life.

Thank you!
Linda Boerstler
July 1, 2019

God gives every bird its food, but He does not throw it into the nest.

J.G. Holland

In this land
Of still water
The grass whispers
With every footfall.

I remember the smell
Of earth and life
Emanating from the forest
Just after a rain.

Sliding down the
Slippery moss covered
Slopes made smooth
By my bottom.

Letting the black silt
From the creek basin
Ooze up between
My naked toes.

Standing knee deep
With rolled up pants
Hair tossed in the wind
Head thrown back in joy.

Laughing uncontrollably
Until every syllable
Joins in the chorus
Filled to life's brim.

By the still waters
I stand and gaze
At my reflection in the pool
And wonder -----

I cannot remember the last time that I was able to go fishing before dawn with my dad. I really don't think that I caught anything other than minnows or other small creatures, but whatever I hooked was quickly returned to the flowing river. In between our conversations I could listen to the changing sounds of night and day and watch the movement of the stars as dawn burst through the darkness. It was a holy time. A time where I felt fully a part of the world around me, and closer to my father than at any time.

In the city in which I live, most of the sounds of nature are obliterated by the constant roar of traffic. In addition, the bright urban lights burn so brightly that the surrounding sky never goes completely dark. Rather, I want to see the muted cerulean sky, clouded with mist and fog that takes me away from any human generated noise so that I can discover the music of the silence. I can only imagine the constellations and remember the sounds from these early mornings when conversations were made with few words and whispers.

In Psalm 23, which is familiar to all, the poet speaks of being led beside the still waters by the shepherd for the purpose of restoring the soul. Soft green pastures encourage one to come and rest, be completely safe, have all of one's needs met, and to lay aside those things that are life draining such as war, diseases, poverty, and the like. When one only focuses on the basics of mere survival life in general becomes drudgery and meaningless. As one grows older things that were important easily fade into the background. It was easy to become wearied in the attempt to obtain things that are tangible and temporary. The most valuable are those things that are intangible because they can be treasured within the confines of the soul and remembered in the deepest part of the heart.

Annotated Psalms 23. KJV

The Lord (the creator of heaven and earth and the lover of my soul), **is my shepherd** *(my caretaker, my provider, the one in whom I can trust).*

I shall not want *(shall not want any of the false and temporary things from the world that have no value, and that tarnish and disintegrate like sand that falls through the fingers of the hand holding it).*

He makes me to lie down in green pastures; *(makes me, not of force or demand, but of sweet invitation and alluring with love and desire, as of great love and affection)*

To lie down *(as in repose, sleep, rest, to pause from senseless activity, in a place of peace, undisturbed, no darkness, unmarred to be perfect, plush and verdant, abundant and no lack, to be in a place where one can thrive).*

He leads me beside the still waters *(he leads but one is given a choice to follow or not follow, to respond to a generous invitation or to ignore it; the leader persuades but does not demand).*

Beside *(he is not in front, nor behind but besides, a denotation of companionship. Clearly the leader will not make another do what he would not do himself).*

The still waters *(a place where there is no turmoil, no exhaustive striving, no suffering, near the calm movement of water that is peaceful, lends to healing and restoration as indicative of Jesus being the "living water" with which the soul would need no other nourishment).*

To restore my soul, *(provide restoration rejuvenation, being made as new and returning it to its original and perfect condition as in being made new or born again).*

He leads me to paths of righteous for his name's sake; (paths, easy going, in such a magical place, like a trail in a well-groomed garden as opposed to one that is rugged, rough and overgrown making passing difficult. Again, denotes easy leading but one must be led because only the leader knows where the path goes, so the follower is dependent).

Righteousness (is more a destination rather than just a word; the condition that one becomes when he or she is restored from an unholy state to a state of holiness which then allows access to the presence of God, in the holy of holies, the place in which God dwelled. It is through the love and kindness of the shepherd, and his will that those who followed him would have the ability to live in His presence forever; a cyclical notion that the green pastures and still waters were found in heaven, where God the shepherd dwells. Righteousness depends on God, not from any effort on the follower except for the choice to follow the leader on the right path).

For his name's sake (if something has someone's name on it, this signifies ownership, such as the fact that the pastures belong to Him because of a transaction to purchase, receive, or create, by way of inheritance or other transference, now being fully owned by the shepherd, as well as the sheep. Livestock, etc. that reside there, and therefore is fully responsible for the care taking and the care giving of the property as well as what that property holds).

The shadow of death (the specter of darkness that hangs over the earth. It is the picture of gloom, loss, and grieving. God in his benevolence knows how foreboding and fearful of the concept of death but his comfort is there to lead, as a shepherd leads his sheep, through the times of affliction, desolation and loss which can be the losing or separation of someone or something that is sentimental, familiar, spiritual, etc. Here the poet reassures that there is no reason for fear or bereavement. Though those be a momentary struggle God restores, replaces and give that which is greater than that that was lost. 1 Corinthians 15: 25-27 KJV).

I will fear no evil *(God is ever there through the light and through the darkness and understands the severe difficulty that ensues. Not only does God accompany the one who suffers, but also offers the tools that are needed to help one get through to the green pastures.*

Surely goodness and mercy shall follow, *(when the seeker pursues and watches for the shepherd who at the same time is watching for them.)*

I will dwell in the house of the Lord forever, *(not just referring to a physical structure but also in the fulfillment of God's promises in full enjoyment of the life of abundance to come.)*

Your rod and your staff comfort (*the flock knows that when they see the rod and the staff, they are near the place that with the shepherd will find safety and peace).*

The table before me, *(depicts an open invitation to the table of abundance which is available to those who believe.)*

In the presence of my enemies, *(when the believers are finally vindicated. The enemies will look at the rewards and the banquet that are presented to the flock. The abundance of God is there because these have chosen Christ and have been faithful to his word.)*

Anointing my head with oil – *(denotes extensive caring by the shepherd. The sheep were anointed daily with oil to protect it from bugs, some which could turn into worms that will burrow into the brain of the animal. Oil was also used to protect the sheep from the aggressiveness of other sheep within the flock; the oil not allowing a sheep to make contact when attempting to bite. Oil also would be* *applied to any wounds suffered from scraping against rock, trees and other hazards.*

In retrospect then, it behooves us, even though it is difficult, to disregard the ravages of aging and decaying of our bodies because as stated by St. Paul in 2 Corinthians 5:17; *"therefore it anyone be in Christ (psalm 23's shepherd) he or she is a new creature, old things are passed away, behold ALL things are become new".* The scars from the wounds received through the battles of life, the reminders of the emotional trauma, the great loss and sorrow will be removed completely, and all things will become new.

Psalm 23 KJV

The Lord is my shepherd;
I shall not want.
He makes me to lie down
In green pastures.
He leads me beside
The still waters.
He restores my soul
He leads me in
The paths of righteousness
For His name's sake.
Yes, though I walk
Through the valley
Of the shadow of death,
I will feel no evil;
For You are with me;
Your rod and your staff,
They comfort me.
You prepare a table before me
In the presence of my enemies;
You anoint my head with oil;
My cups run over.
Surely goodness and mercy
Shall follow me
All the days of my life.

If I had faith
Maybe I could believe
That men are trees walking
That mud heals blindness
And that dead people live.

Maybe I could trust
That I would receive what I asked for
Have plenty of bread and fish
And walk on water.

If I believed
Maybe I'd stop bleeding
Or be able to walk again
Or survive a shipwreck.

If I had hope
Then I could wait
For His coming in the clouds
To draw me to himself.

But faith is hard work
And though there is a
Faint scent of hope
I am hard-pressed to set
My soul in that direction.

How do I take the concept of faith and define it in a personal way that is indicative of my own relationship with God and with the world? Many people believe that they must feel the presence of God near them in order to know what He exists. They are high maintenance needing to have the touch, the warmth, the guiding of the hand or all else is lost. When one is young in the faith, Christ manifests Himself in ways that are vital and exciting. The newest believers feel close to their God and to each other because the strength of the community is necessary for them to grow into maturity. They are like very active children who what to be close to their parents at all time. We want to be close to God.

As we grow older the "feelings" of faith become more elusive. Times come upon us that make us question our faith. Suddenly, we don't feel like God is close to us anymore and we become more dependent not only with the knowledge in our heads but also what we sense with respect to the importance of our faith from previous experiences. In the darkest part of the night we must hold on to the little light that we have, because we know that someday the morning will come again, whether it be on this side of the river or the other.

The knowledge of God, even when He is distant, or when I am distant, is what sustains me. I live this life in full anticipation of eternity. If I were in a night that was never followed by day, there would be no point in continuing. Suffering is only made acceptable at its worst because we know that it is a temporary situation. When God is at the end of the road, no matter how rough the journey, the destination is glorious.

In my mind I keep telling myself that if I can endure ten minutes of suffering, I can enjoy an eternity of peace. Sometimes if you get close enough you can see some of the light peeking through that glimmer of hope. That helps us to know that we are only visitors on this planet. Our citizenship is in heaven. It changes the perspective of life when you realize that this temporal world which seems to be permanent is less than a whisper when compared with eternity.

I know that I often live as if I have no faith; that I am thinking about things that are far from being spiritual or mystical. I am not able to empty myself out because the world keeps hurling itself at me and as a result I am forced to live and fight within it. This expends my lifeblood and I end up fighting for lesser things that I believe will insure my survival. But truly, what is it that I am surviving for if my goal and destination remains to the other side where everything of value begins and ends?

It drives me –this faith – this knowledge of God's presence within me and around me. I have had so many things and people soundly ripped from me that I have felt much like an amputee with a missing limb. At times when I am up preparing to go to work, I find myself thinking, "what if I die today?" I watch things happen in front of me and behind me on the freeway. It isn't a sad thought except for the consideration of the possible consequences of the carnage but, it is the promise of faith that pushes through despite the great fear.

For someone to have no faith in God is for someone to be already dead to themselves. Life is meaningless and the only thing to look forward to is the end of it when whatever is perceived as this current and present misery ceases once and for all. There is an anticipation of nothing – hoping that the mere emptiness of nothingness, of no life or existence becomes that eternal relief from all the horrid things of like. Why would someone want to live eternally in the present state, on in their current condition? Why would someone choose to prolong the agony, the endless and miserable pain by just being alive? Why subject one's self to more suffering, hurting and disappointment? No, it is better to be dead to not have to feel or care at all. But my faith tells me that through Christ everything changes.

There is no turning back. Even when I lived my life as a pagan my faith never died. Even when I lived in immorality, I knew God was there. I knew he was there I knew he was there when I purposely placed myself in some seriously dangerous situations. He was there despite me. He protected me from those who might have intended to do me harm. I don't know the reason for this except for the expression of His great love for me.

The accompanying Psalm discusses this topic but there is also a twist to it. There is a propensity for one to seek solace in our fellow human beings, especially our family and friends. There is no denial that God often brings people in that can offer comfort as well as a solution for the present situation. Options can be made clear that weren't there before. However, one needs to exercise caution because friends can also misguide, lead one into the wrong decision, give one the wrong advice, or even become insistent that they know the specific details of the trouble that is being faced. Care should also be taken that the advisor is not upset because either the seeker has chosen to not follow the advice or in following the given advice the solution is not the one expected.

Psalm 55 KJV (annotated)
Give ear to my prayer, O God, (Listen to me, God)

And *do not hide Yourself* from my supplication. (Make yourself known to me so that I see you are listening)

Attend to me and hear me; (pay attention to what I am telling you)

I am restless in my complaint, and moan noisily, (cannot settle in the silence, and cannot stop the pain)

Because of the voice of the enemy, (the enemy allows me no peace)

Because of the oppression of the wicked; (the wicked are set out to silence me)

For they bring down trouble upon me, (I am overwhelmed by them)

And in wrath they hate me. (there is no love nor compassion)

My heart is severely pained within me, (the emotional pain is too much)

And the terrors of death have fallen upon me. (am I going to die?)

Fearfulness and trembling have come upon me, (am so scared that I am visibly shaking)

And horror has overwhelmed me. (I have no control over the power of hell)

So, I said, "Oh, that I had wings like a dove! (Oh God set me free from this evil)

I *would fly away* and be at rest. (in hiding where no one can find me).

Indeed, *I would wander far* off, (far, far from this horrible place)

And remain in the wilderness. (So, I can dwell in God's house forever) *Selah*

I would hasten my *escape* (cannot get away from here fast enough).

From the windy *storm and tempest*." (there is no protection or shelter)

Destroy, O Lord, *and* *divide* their tongues, (Destroy and break their alliances)

For I have seen violence and strife *in the city*. (It is too close to me)

Day and night, *they go around* it on its walls; (I am surrounded by them)

Iniquity and trouble *are* also during *it*

Oppression and deceit *depart not* from its streets. (the youth and the children follow them)

For *it is* **not an enemy** *who* reproaches me; (I know them and live with them)

Then I could *bear it*. (these are my friends, we understood each other)

Nor *is it* one *who* hates me who has *exalted himself* against me; (how could they betray me like this? I thought they loved me)

Then I could **hide from him.** (I cannot hide because all the hiding places are known)

But *it was **you***, a man my ***equal***, (we work together and played on the same team)

My ***companion*** and my acquaintance. (we have known each other since childhood)

We took sweet **counsel** together, (and what about all the plans we made?)

*And **walked*** to the house of God in the throng. (we walked with God together as brothers)

Let ***death*** seize them; (if they choose death instead of life, let them die)

Let them go ***down alive into hell***, (I cannot believe that they treated me this way, I am done with them).

For **wickedness** *is* in their dwellings *and* among them. (they never told me the truth; I trusted them)

As for me***, I will call upon God,*** (if I must stand alone with God then so be it)

And the L ORD ***shall save me***. (He will save me and protect me from all harm)

Evening and morning and at noon (I am never alone nor am I forsaken)

I will ***pray,*** and cry ***aloud***, (I am not ashamed to say His name so that all can hear)

And He shall ***hear*** my voice. (He hears me! He knows me! He loves me!)

He has **redeemed my soul** in peace from the battle *that was* against me, (He purchased me with his own blood, I am solely His)

For there were many **against me**. (everyone I know)

God will **hear**, and **afflict** them, (God has seen their misdeeds and the condition of their heart)

Even He who **abides from of old**. (does not matter how long ago they maligned you, they have not gone unnoticed)

Because *they* **do not change**, (they cannot change of their own afford)

Therefore, **they do not fear God**. (they live as if God doesn't exist)

He has put forth his hands against those who were at peace with him; (He has convinced others to also betray him)

He has **broken** his covenant. (because they have decided to not honor the promises that they had made to God)

The words of his mouth were smoother than butter, (people believed him just because he manipulated them)

But **war was in his heart**; (a wolf in sheep's clothing, desiring to deceive and devour)

His words **softer than oil**, (persuasive, compassionate, generous, loving)

Yet they *were* drawn were **swords**. (His only goal was to cut, destroy, mislead and capture them for his own purpose or control)

Cast your burden on the LORD, (God does not expect you to carry the heavy load of demands on you)

And *He shall sustain* you; (God will carry you and your burdens)

He shall *never permit the righteous* to be moved. (no other entity or person have the authorization to circumvent God's plan)

But You, O God, shall bring them down to *the pit of destruction;* (they will not benefit from their evil doings)

Bloodthirsty and deceitful men *shall not live out half their days;* (for God will cut them off from eternal life)

But I will trust in you. (and dwell in the House of God forever.)

Calm me
Hold me
Within thine arms
Enfold me.
Do not forsake
My broken heart.
My prayer O Lord
May thy love impart
Protect the longings
Of my soul,
Shield me God
And make me whole.

Save me for I am frail.
Help me now
So, I cannot fail.
This world I live in
Leaves me frightened,
O Christ, my savior
My darkness heightened.

I am alone and
I am lost.
The storm is fierce
And I am tossed
Back and forth
Like crumbled leaves.
Assist me God
I am in great need.

May my prayers be heard
Within the crying.
The pain is great!
I feel I'm dying.
Unless you help me
There is no denying
That I am heading
To the great abyss.
I beg you please
Save me from this.

Have mercy God
On me a sinner.
Have mercy God
On me a sinner.

When I was young, I was fearful of storms. Here in the Midwest I was forced to face that fear more often than I would have liked. There was always something fierce in the approaching storm front, formidable wall clouds and the heightened sense of power from something bigger than me. How I feared the twisting, boiling sky, yellow high-pressure atmosphere, before the first strike of lightning.

I remember an experience from summer camp when I was a teen that I will never forget. Our group was involved in some activities from the dining hall a bit of distance from our unit. We slept in what were called takins, which were part canvas tent and part cabin making it a semi-permanent structure. As a rule, because of the hot and humid summer days, the canvas sides were rolled up and tied to catch any hint of a breeze.

We could hear a storm brewing up in the distance and knew that all the canvas flaps were tied wide-open. We ran as quickly as possible to get to the tebins before the full force of the storm hit. As we ran down the rocky path there was a huge strike of lightning and then a very loud crash. As it was behind me, I kept running, now because of fear instead of the haste in which I started.

As I glanced over my shoulder, I was shocked to discover that right in the path, right in the middle of my dash up the slope a tree had fallen in response to the very loud crash. It was not a large tree, but it lay about two steps behind the very spot where I heard the crash. I could have been struck by that tree. With a shriek, I was moving faster than I ever had in my life, either before or after. I got to the safety of the tebins and pulled down the flaps and fastened them.

Moving forward some decades later I know that a storm excites me. I am fascinated by the advance of the rolling crowds and the darkening of the sky. I love the different smell in the air as the sun peers through the channels of clouds. When the lightning blasts through the dark making it as bright as daylight for a split second, and the thunder responses like a low and heavy slapping wave I am thrilled.

Then the rain comes like a curtain, a wall of water as it quickly washes everything around me. As it is with most of these spring and summer storms, they are fierce and strong but short-lived, ending as quickly as they begin leaving behind broken branches and other damage, and flooded drains and street.

I have been fortunate to have never been through something as dramatic as a hurricane, but I have seen pictures of the aftermath. It reminds me that God is sovereign and determined in his course of action. God speaks and moves as He chooses needing no authorization or permission to do so. To us, the devastation is a random and certain event and we are unable to contrive explanations as to why. It is not my purpose to defend God or to offer answers to questions that we all have. Things are as they are and a quick reading from the Old Testament book of Job is a description of God's ordering of the universe and those that live within it.

Job 36: 26 – 35 KJV (annotated)
How great is God beyond our **understanding**? (We are incapable of knowing him fully).

The number of his years is past our finding out. (God has no beginning and no end).

He draws up the drops of water which distill as rain to the streams, (He gathers all unto himself)

the clouds pour down their moisture and **abundantly showers mankind**. (He is no respecter of persons)

Who can understand **how** He spreads out the clouds? (all things are orchestrated by him)

See how He scatters his lightning about him (no one can duplicate His power).

and **covers the depths** of the sea. (the water flows as an indication of His living water).

This is the **way he governs** the nations (God needs no defense or explanation for what he does. He is sovereign).

and provides his food in **abundance**. (abundance means that there is always more than enough).

He **fills his hands** with lightning (by his outstretched arms).

and **commands** it to strike its mark. (he directs all the movements of the earth).

His thunder announces the coming storm - - (There is no other besides He)

The **cattle also**, concerning the rising storm – (even the cattle respond to Him)

Job 36: 26 – 33 KJV
Behold, God is great, and we do not know him; nor can the number of His years be discovered. For He draws up drops of water, which distill as rain from the mist, which the clouds drop down and pour abundantly on man. Indeed, can anyone understand the spreading of clouds, the thunder from His canopy? Look He scatters His light upon it and covers the depths of the sea. For by these He judges the peoples; He gives food in abundance. He covers His hands with lightning and commands it to strike. His thunder declares it. The cattle also concerning the rising storm.

Rising again

The rose blooms red.
Soft petals form
In the winter's dream.
Long past the storm;
And when the spring
Bursts from the tomb.
The blushing bud
Emerges from the womb.

The touch of a hand
Pure and divine
Began the root
Before the start of time
And knew the thorns
It carries now
To be the ones
Forced upon his brow.

Blood crimson dripped
Upon his head
All heaven knew
He would soon be dead
From wounds pierced
Through his holy skin.
No one could tell
The love within.

Red rose, red rose
Blooming upon the bush
With velvet petals –
He made you first.
Beauty can only
Come from pain
And only Son shine
Can still the rain.

The hardest part of getting older is the realization that your abilities and mobility has declined and that you can't continue to do the things that you did in your youth. For example; staying up all night and being effective the next day or coming home from your job completely exhausted counting the hours until you can go to bed heralds the fact that you are no longer twenty years old. In addition, you can tell that it takes longer for you to recover from an illness or your thought processes are not as quick and sharp as they used to be.

Still it is a tough thing to acknowledge and face. The adage, "old age is not for sissies," is appropriate here. And to watch the decline of those whom you love, such as your parents or grandparents is equally as difficult to deal with. Our parents, in most cases, are the ones that taught us about relationships. You had to learn that an acquaintance is someone which whom you interact with or a daily basis but will not likely develop into a lasting friendship. This person might be a coworker or a classmate or someone you talk to in other social settings but would not necessarily acknowledge him or her out of the place that you most have things in common, as in work, or a school environment. An enduring relationship runs deeper in that both of you will maintain a relationship that is lasting but not necessarily familial.

Then there is the unconditional relationship that we all long for. Some are fortunate enough to find this type of relationship within the family unit, from parents, siblings, grandparents, etc. Others have not had that exposure due to a tumultuous childhood. These relationships come from those who are the most prominent in your life and upbringing. They have a greater impact on not only your life but with the development of you at your core, personality, interaction but also respect, encouragement, and the willingness to be helpful to others, even those whom you do not know. A child may have deduced that his or her parents are always there and will be there when others are not. That is a very strong connection.

In a poem written by William Cowper the importance of that deep and familial relationship is represented;

What peaceful hours I once enjoyed/how sweet the memory still/but they have left an aching void/the world can never fill. The implication here is that while other people and things may temporarily ease that longing. This is an angst and an emptiness inherent in very person. The longing is like that of having an unquenchable thirst, in the middle of the desert where no water is.

The further comparison would be that of the blooming rose, vibrant, soft, a sense of comfort, during a bramble that is fierce and has destructive thorns. One may desire to possess the rose in its

Exquisite beauty but because of the long thorns, cannot obtain it. Many are not willing to take the risk to reach into the bramble just to pluck that rose from its thin stem. Getting to the roses means that one must accept the danger to life and limb and perhaps the possibility of death.

Jesus is the rose within the thorns. He possesses and eternal beauty far more appealing than that of the rose. There is one narrow way of accessibility and that is through the wicked thorns. That is the only way we can get to him. Drawing closer we can see that he has blood on his face, nails in his hands and feet and with the skin of his back ripped and painful beyond imagine due to the flogging he must endure.

He placed himself into an untenable wilderness to show us that even in the direst of places hope is not and never will be lost. Because he stood in the middle of the thorns, he was not able to embrace us. His extravagant love for us meant that he sustained through extreme suffering, so that we would not have to even to the point of death. This rose bruised and torn beyond recognition did not let the brambles and the thorns contain it. The love for us was too strong and he was compelled to get to us. Because he did this with supreme effort and sacrifice to make a place for us were, we can be removed from all grief and pain, where we, like that rose will never die or fade.

Romans 8: 28-30 –KJV (annotated)

and I am **convinced** (persuaded, determined, made up my mind)

that **nothing** (no substitute)

can **ever** (eternal, no end, forever),

separate (come in between, take away, stop),

from **God's love**. (there is no love that is greater than this).

Neither **death nor life** (death is the beginning of life for those in Christ).

neither **angels or demons** (good or evil),

neither our **fears** (doubts, worry and disbelief)

for today nor our worries about tomorrow; **not even the power of hell** (God is all powerful. Consider this, that for us who are in Christ, the current life in which we live will be our only hell, and when we die, we will be in heaven. For those who are not in Christ, the life in which they live now will be their only heaven, because hell is waiting for them)

can (cannot prevail against God's love)
separate us from God's love.

No (nothing from heaven or earth can possibly go against the power of God)

power in the sky above or from the earth below – {[indeed nothing in all creation will ever be able to separate us from the love of God that is revealed in Christ Jesus our Lord.]

Think of yourself as an incandescent power, illuminated and perhaps forever talked to by God and His messengers.

Brenda Ireland

Haikus of celebration

I celebrate life
Jumping up like spring mornings
Full of love and freshness.

Yes, there are dark clouds
And deep heavy shadows
But the sun still shines.

I celebrate breath
Full lung filling inhalations
Of fragrance and joy.

And vision, pure and clear
Seeing things as if I have
Never seen them before.

I celebrate love
As it was meant to be
Praised, embraced, touched.

Evoking laughter
But also evoking tears
And great sorrow.

I celebrate creation
Like a small flower
Blooming for the first time.

And the hope for peace
In the ballet of eternity
And in the heart of God.

Most of my life I suffered little or no physical pain. I went through my days like a runaway train and tried to convince myself that I needed little sleep. If I had any pain at all it was usually a result of some injury or other and I would just push through pretend that it didn't exist. I would not let anyone, or anything stop me. Once the wound or injury healed it was like it didn't happen at all.

Emotional pain is a far different story. For me physical pain is just a result of being alive and human. It was far easier to deal with than emotional pain. A hurting soul or a broken heart causes wounding that is far deeper and devastating. When a friend betrays me, for example, it is as if I were stabbed in the heart. When I have had to suffer with continual emotional and mental abuse, I felt like the only relief that afforded me was death. Many times, I prayed that I could just to fall asleep and not wake up again. When I am going through the worst of it, I feel as if I am alone.

I came into this world small and perfect with the potential of doing anything I would ever want to do. I believed that I had a lifetime of blessings, dreams and promises. When I was in my youth, I believed that all things were possible. I believed it because I didn't know otherwise; it all seemed very clear to me. I believed that I could jump to the moon and back and oversee the universe. Everything I saw was beautiful and everything I touched was gold. As far as I was concerned, I had no limitations or restrictions. I was told that my dreams were senseless, and my gifting was a figment of my own imagination. I did not yet know that imagination was just a ruse or a terrible joke. No one led me to think that what I envisioned was impossible.

So, I conformed to the restlessness and the despondency of normal life. It was my thinking that made me wish for things that I did not already have. The motto then was "if you work hard enough and long enough," what you desire will come to you. No one told me that it would take a lifetime to get to that point, and, and that many don't finish the race. How disappointed I was when I discovered that dreams were just that, "dreams." Searching for a far way place with fruit trees, bluebirds and unicorns was useless, because such a place did not exist.

I became consumed by the work and endless labor. I was so consumed that I lost the vision of the original plan. The time I spent dreaming was now spent in just trying to survive, shelter and sustain myself from day to day. I have lost track of the original pathway and am wandering around so lost that I fear that I will never get home again. "Blessings" in my opinion were not a regular thing so for the most part I had nothing to look forward to. One day was very much like the one before. Soon it felt like my life was just one never-ending and impossible day that I wish that would someday be over. Where was the break, the joy, the beauty and peace that I thought I would find at the beginning of my journey? Now everything seemed to be illusive and nonsensical.

I began to believe what others told me or exhibited. Nothing really mattered anymore and beyond that, if it did matter no one would give a damn. This then became my journey to nowhere and nothing. This alone caused me mental confusion. The harder I worked to understand and make sense of things the more confused I became. The truth is that nothing on this earth makes sense, and no matter how long I pondered about it, nothing would change.

So, I stopped searching. I stopped trying to figure things out. I stopped expecting for things to be different. This took an emotional toll on me. I didn't know where to invest my emotions and effort. The loss, the rejection, closed my emotions so that I could not feel. I functioned like a robot in struggles that did nothing but destroy me. I had no point, no purpose, and seemingly, no future. I had lost any enthusiasm and motivation. I did not know what, who, why, I was suffering the emotional and mental stress continually.

I have been a peregrine without a home, flying from place to place to find where I could belong, accepted and welcomed. I only found the rocks and deserts. I would climb upwards and then downward in an endless struggle hoping that the solution to my problems was just on the other side of the mountain. I only found more desolation and hopelessness.

Life is nothing but a journey and never intended for me to settle in; never intended for me to sit on my laurels and expect everything and everyone around me to fulfill my dreams. I expected too much from others and realized that if I was going to accomplish something I could never stop moving forward. Surrendering to no forward movement at all caused something to die inside. Looking back was not at option either because in doing so I was forced to relive the failures and the heartaches. Things are always more destructive when the anger and the hurt replays over and over. I had to accept "my lot" in life. Even though there had been times of darkness and great uncertainty I had no time to stop and moan about it. Moving forward, seeking what was in front of me was my only way of survival. Though others would try and stop me and stand in my way to circumvent any progress that I had made, I had to shut out the noise. To fall in the negativity in others would only lead me to a place of no return; a place in which I could not escape or recover.

We are not residents of this planet. This earth is just a stopping place. Things that we try to use or possess only hampers the original purpose of our lives. We become unable to see what is ahead. Instead we prefer to wallow in our sorrows, blame others, and yell at God because it has all been so unfair. Why can't He be easy on us instead of making things difficult and impossible? We do the best we can with the little that we start with by squandering and misusing what we were given. We tromp on them thinking that we can find something better. How is it that we, the creature, know more than God, the creator, believe that we care better managers of our own affairs than He is? We are simply frustrating ourselves when we think to do things our way when God has already made a pathway for us. It's always there in plain sight. We are just too wrapped up in ourselves to see it.

Certainly, we can avoid most of the emotional stress and mental anxiety by not making things harder than they need to be. It was easy for me to get too enmeshed with the small things that I could not see the big things. We believe in God but for some reason we have made him too small to handle our disasters and catastrophes.

My journey is still long and hard and exhausting. There will still be steep mountains to climb and oceans to navigate. But the joy in this is that he is with us. We don't have to go it alone. We don't have to climb every obstacle. We don't have to walk in the darkness and with that the pain becomes easier to bear and thinking clear. The physical pain is just there because we are humans in frail bodies and are limited by them. It won't be so hard if we pay attention to it, move in liberty within it, and rejoice through the rest of it.

Vs 1 the **fire [of God]** came down from heaven – *specifically states where the fire of God comes from. This consumed the burnt offering and the sacrifices. (fire of God = power of God = presence of God). The sacrifices were worthy of God to receive, the fire a theophany of God; not only was God in the fire but was the fire. (for it was pleasing to God)*

Vs 2 **priests could not enter** *(because the fire was intense and consuming, and the house (the holy of holies)* **was filled with the glory and presence of God.**

Vs 3 **all the children) of Israel** *(God's fire included people from the 12 tribes of Israel)* bowed down with their faces to the ground (no one is able to see God and live but his glory and presence filled the house so, they worshipped him).

V 5 **King Solomon offered for his sacrifice** *(22,000 oxen and 120,000 sheep, indicative of his wealth and favor from God)* dedicated to the house of God.

V 6 **Priests waited** (for their time to serve).

V 7 **musical instruments** *(used specifically for the worship of God in the house; all Israel stood when these instruments made by David were used in worship).*

V 8 **Solomon hallowed the middle of the court** *(setting it apart signifying that it was built for this purpose; for the offerings, burnt offerings, fat of the peace offering to replace the original altar as it was not adequate).*

V 7 **Solomon kept the feasts (***which he had done before)* with the whole population of Israel *(boundaries from Hamath to the river of Egypt).*

V 10 8th day for **the dedication of the altar** and 7 days for the feasts *(total 14 days of celebration),* 23rd day **people sent home** to their own tents rejoicing in the goodness of God to David and Solomon.

2 Chronicles 7: 1 - 10

Now when Solomon had made an end of praying, the fire came down from heaven and consumed the burnt offering and the sacrifices; and the glory of the Lord filled the house. And the priests could not enter then the house of the Lord, because the glory of the Lord filled the house. And when all the children of Israel saw how the fire came down, and the glory of the Lord upon their house, they bowed themselves with their faces to the ground, and worshipped and praised the Lord saying, "For He is good and his mercy endured forever."

Then the King and all the people offered sacrifices before the Lord. And King Solomon offered a sacrifice of 22,000 oxen, and 120,000 sheep; so, the King and all the people dedicated the house of God.

And the priests waited on their office; the Levites also with instruments of music of the Lord because His mercy endured forever. When David praised by their ministry, and the priests sounded trumpets bef0re them, and all Israel stood. Moreover, Solomon hallowed the middle of the court, and the fat of the offerings, because the brazen altar which Solomon has made was not able to receive the burnt offering, and the meat of the offerings and the fat.

Also, at the time Solomon kept the seven feast days, and all Israel with him, a very great congregation from the entering in of Hamath unto the river of Egypt. And in the eighth day the made a solemn assembly; for they kept the dedication of the altar seven days, and the feast seven days.

And on the third and twentieth day of the 7th month, he sent the people away into their tents, glad and merry in heart for the goodness that the Lord had shewed unto David, and to Solomon, and to Israel His people.

I do not know my purpose
I never had a plan
Mostly I just keep wandering
In this strange and unknown land
Always on the lookout
For something I cannot see.
What is it that I was made for?
Why was I made to be?

Flowers bloom in springtime.
The fall brings colored leaves.
The winter comes with snowfall.
The summer comes with breeze.
Every note belongs to a song
And every word a page.
But I am lost and stand alone,
Confused and much afraid.

Someday before my time is o'er
And my walk on earth is done,
Shed a light to show me reasons
Why I never found the one
True purpose for my living
And why you gave me birth?
I am too old to wander
To finally find my worth.

My journey always undefined.
I have no guide or map
To lead me on the dusty way
Maybe someone saw a ray
Of my shining hope and faith
To which even in the dark I clung
As I slowly kept the pace.

Continuing the journey is fraught with frustration when there are no maps; no paths or no scout to go ahead to place markers pointing to a destination. The destination is the same for everyone, however, there is only one straight and narrow path and Jesus is the only one that knows the way. If we trust Him, the way may not be easier, but the traveler can be comforted in the knowledge that she does not travel alone. We must move forward blindly and try to navigate by the prompting of the Holy Spirit. If we can listen above the growing noise from the world, we will hear his voice to lead us.

Something is required by all that embark on such a trip. Prior to departure the tools have been given in preparation; life, breath, intelligence, love, beauty and so much more. These are available for all pilgrims. Most of our lives are spent attempting to uncover the reason for which we are created. Some are fortunate enough to find what they are looking for, their calling, and can have their dreams fulfilled early on in live. Others, like myself, every day is a struggle, many obstacles are ahead; most of which are self-manufactured because of wrong decisions and choices. There are many wrong turns causing us to have to backtrack and start over. Things may seem clear and straightforward at the beginning, but it isn't long before the for rolls in. Soon the way is muddled, rugged, impossible and it seems that it is difficult to make any forward progress. This becomes wearisome and discouraging.

It is in those times, the dark times, that the temptation is to disregard the calling and to venture off the path. Surely there is an easier way, right? How easy it is for one to be distracted and pulled away from the original plan. Perhaps there is an attraction to others who have forged their own trail, thinking that they know more than the Master of Construction. Perhaps one will be drawn to a sparkling bauble that can be seen but beyond reach. Perhaps there has been great loss, devastation, illness and betrayal.

There can be many obstructions that can make one doubt the direction of the journey. The strength comes when the things, people, places, etc., are ignored and one chooses to stay on the write path. Greater reward waits ahead because of the faithfulness and the determination to not turn to the right or to the left. It may not seem that there is any profit in the effort. However, it is it very difficult to stay on course and very easy to drift away from the goal.

For those who struggle, life is a paradox. One knows the value of staying on course but there is always justification that supports the need to stray. Surely nothing would be lost in temporary exploration. One can always go back, retrace the steps, and get back on the path. Unfortunately, many do not get back to where they were, too much time is lost. There are many things that are delightful and colorful which will always pique the curiosity and the desire to possess.

The thing is, there is nothing in this world that could give more than momentary satisfaction. There is nothing that we can lay our hands on that will not be destroyed – there are no treasures on earth. It is only in heaven that we can find the finest, unflawed jewel. That is where we should be looking.

I believe that God wants us to have the desires of our heart. He knows what fills that aching longing that persists in the deepest chambers of our soul. He knows the eternal and it is He that urges us to stay on the right path. We are not citizens of this planet. Our citizenship is in heaven. We might not find our find our calling or purpose on earth, but will we see how things flow together when we are standing next to the throne.

When we mourn, He mourns with us. He is the kind Father who wants to give his children good and lasting things; treasures that he has created and saved specifically for us. When we receive those treasures given by His own hand, the journey will make sense. All the questions will be answered, and all the bruises will be healed. God does not just want to give us heaven, His kingdom residence. He is generous and His purpose, his dream, is that we all reside with him so that we can be what he created us to be. We are heirs of things that we never dreamed of and beyond anything we can ask for or think of.

So, what does God require of us? What is our purpose, our dream? It's very simple. All He wants is for us to believe, to know he is real, and he loves. He is generous and his purpose, his dream, is that we all reside with him.

Annotated

He has shown you – *God has already made known what He requires. The problems come when we act as though He has not.*

What is good – *all good things come from Him, for he is a Father that loves his children.*

Do justly – *treat all people the same, with fairness, kindness, and compassion.*

Love mercy – *God is merciful in that He doesn't give us what we deserve, because we deserve nothing; his mercy gifts us with grace, that He demonstrated with the death of His beloved Son on the cross and showed the victory over death with His resurrection.*

Walk humbly – *to be unpretentious, to be aware of one's position, to be meek, not to draw attention to oneself but to demonstrate dependence on God for all things. To not be conceited, haughty, condescending or rude and to treat the Janitor with the same respect as one would treat the CEO.*

Micah 6:8

He has shown you, O man, what is good; and what does the Lord require of you but, to do justly, to love mercy, and to walk humbly with your God?

In the beginning

Before the inception of time,
Before the breath of God brooded
Like a shimmering mist over the deep,
Before the stars knew their places
Or the first fiery finger of golden sunset
Its illumination through the dark,
You were! Your name softly whispered
From the mouth of the Creator.

The sparkle of life birthed by Great Love who
Caressed the very thought of you, over and over.
Choosing face, and eyes and voice.
And family and place and time.
Before the first bloom of exuberant petal
On slender stem, the subtle fragrance embracing
The first kiss of dew on the young grass
Before the first note of birdsong, you were!
And for you He made the world.

God sees the beginning and the ending at the same time. He sees all the time in the middle as well. He is not limited by man's concept of time. To us, keeping time, is crucial in our daily lives. Our days are regimented by deadlines, and schedule, and seasons, and years. We are young and then we are old. We must crawl out of bed at a certain time so we can be at work in time. While at work we handle deadlines, and over time, and lunch time. We mark the passing of time through birthdays and other significant events.

We can only see the segment of time in which we are amid, and then it is a moment by moment, second by second event. We all try to project into the future, and sometimes in the past, ignoring the present moment. Those moments are precious and should be cherished because they will not happen again. The fact of the matter is the because we are so concerned about the past, which we cannot change, or the future, which we cannot control those valuable moments are missed and gone forever.

When facing a crisis, we call out to God as if, like us, didn't see it coming. But God knew that we were going to face that catastrophe, on he knew that specific day, at this time, in this year. He knew before we were born. He knew our names, our personalities, the characteristics that make us individuals, etc.

Not only that, but God, as the skilled potter that he is, shaped us into form, and placed us in a world made specifically for us.

God is the lover of our soul. He receives great joy when he is about to wrap us in his extravagant love. We are the center of His world, His creation. We are never far from His mind, and even when we lay awake in the darkest part of night, He is there and covers us with his eternal love. In Psalm 139 it tells us that God made all the delicate, inner parts of our body and knit us together in our mother's womb.

The psalmist writes;" thank you for making me so wonderfully complex! Your workmanship is marvelous – how well I know it. You watched me as I was being formed in seclusion, as I was woven together in the dark of the womb. You saw me before I was born. Every day of my life was recorded in your book. Every moment was laid out before a single day had passed. How precious are your thoughts about me, O God, they cannot be numbered."

Psalm 139: 13 – 17 KJV annotated.

You **formed**; *(as a potter would form a vessel from a lump of clay)*

inward parts; *(a piece of art, delicately created, even the inward parts that no one sees)*

knitted me together; *(stitch by stitch, carefully planned, fusing multiple parts to make something of the whole)*

in my mother's womb; *(this is where it all comes together, bit by bit until the child is born, fully human from the beginning).*

I praise you; *(the human body is delicate and strong at the same time. Psalmist praises God for his complexity of life).*

I am **fearfully and wonderfully**

made; *(not thrown together by an explosion, not germinated from a seed, not evolved from a lesser being, but made in God's image, by His own hand, carefully executed and constructed).*

Wonderful are your works *(speaks of the creation, God created the earth, the flora and the fauna,*

My soul knows it very well *(speaking of his response to God's creation, as a created being)*

My frame was not hidden from you *(God the artist created human flesh, from nothing, the beginning, so that God knows every intricate part of the body intimately)*

When I was made in secret *(all of creation was not revealed until God commanded it, no one knew that they existed until they existed, any foreknowledge of creation was only known by the creator).*

Intricately woven in the depths of the earth *(God created the heavens above, the earth below, the depths of the sea, and the creatures that were to live on earth. There was nothing until God brought everything to existence).*

Your eyes saw me before I was formed *(before God created us, we were products of his imagination, he knew what he was going to do before he did it).*

In your book were written every one of them *(this was not necessarily the Book of Life, it was instead The Book of the Living, the name of every creature, every tree, every animal, every human, which can point again to His Imagination)*

The days that were formed for me *(God knows the date we are born, and he knows the day when we die, he assigns everyone their "numbers of days "which signify the length of time they have on earth.*

When yet there were none of them *(God foreknew what would be before it was)*

How precious to me are your thoughts, O God *(the Psalmist expresses his gratefulness for the fact that God thought of him, shows an intimate relationship with God)*

How fast are the sum of them; *(God's thoughts are unknowable to man, so vast they are that there is no beginning and no end.*

Psalm 139: 13 -17 KJV;

For you formed my inward parts; you knitted me together in my mother's womb. I praise you for I am fearfully and wonderfully made. Wonderful are your works; my soul knows it very well. My frame was not hidden from you when I was made in secret, intricately woven in the depths of the earth. Your eyes saw my unformed substance; in your book were written, every one of them. How precious to me are your thoughts, O God! How vast is the sum of them?

Sanctify Ye a Fast

Today I will fast from selfishness
And repent for the many times
That I have put myself first
At the expense of another.
I will seek to meet the needs
Of others even though it may
Cause a great inconvenience for me.
I will lay down my life for a friend.

Today I will fast from idleness
And look forward to giving myself
For the eternal kingdom of God.
I will push away the desire
To be lazy and alone
And find the company
Of those who need my help
And those who need my presence.

Today I will fast from worry
The constant fear of failure
Either on my part, or of another
There will be no wringing of hands
No self-induced stress
No disappointment because
Someone did not do things
As I had expected.

Today I will fast from complacency
For no longer noticing when
The same sun rises every day.
I will not ignore the rush
Of winter wind within my parka.

I will not turn my head when
I see someone else in need
Or pretend as if God doesn't exist.

Today I will fast from prayerlessness
A most needful activity.
That is too often ignored for reasons
Of procrastination or excuse
I will not try to always speak, rather
I will listen for his quiet voice
And I will know not to leave that spot
Until he touches me and blesses me.

Fasting is a spiritual practice that is widely overlooked in today's world. I am not just talking about skipping meals though that it very useful. I am talking about fasting from things that interfere from our relationship with God. In the Old Testament there was much discussion about idols, i.e., worshipping the golden calf for instance, striving for personal power and not relying on the power of God, from which all strength and power come from, or seeking assistance from someone other than God, (in the sense of the occult and other very negative things). If done with the right motives in mind, fasting can be an extremely powerful tool to strengthen the relationship with God, as it is forsaking the cravings of the flesh and focuses on the life of the Holy Spirit within us. God did not design our bodies to go without food for long periods of time. Eating sensibly helps us to maintain our physical health and sustains us. There are those who fasted throughout the Bible, but generally was for a specific reason or purpose.

This however is not the purpose for this writing to discuss the activity of fasting.

Suffice it to say, that anything can be a detriment to our Christian walk, if not done with and for the right reasons. Additionally, there are other things that can be misused, or manipulated for the individual purpose. Anything put above God, that pushes him aside, or disregarded is idolatry. The career in which you are engaged can be, and has been, an obstacle between him or her, that shifts the focus back to human desires and flesh. Simply put, to exchange God, for a higher position or salary, a bigger house, a pretentious job, or the desire to live in a specific neighborhood, could interfere with the ability to know the true will of God, in our lives.

Sometimes, God will call us aside, remove all the things that occupy and distract us, and put us in a place where there is nothing to depend on, to trust in, other than He alone. If called to do this, doing so with strengthen your faith and confidence in the Lord in more ways that you can imagine, if you are diligent and truthful with him.

It has been said that a loving parent will chastise their errant child when he or she has made a mistake.

The chastening can seem harsh to the recipient. However, when that child becomes an adult, he or she will know that the chastening was for their benefit and always done by the hand of love. God will chastise His own, not because he is a mean and dreadful being but because he wants to correct his children so that they could become the person that He created them to be. God gives us every possible way for us to succeed. God does not want his children to suffer from bad decisions and choices, but we must choose to follow his voice. He does not force us.

God's love is far reaching, it is unconditional, and it is eternal. It is not that he doesn't allow us to "be what he wants us to be," it's that he desires for you to be the best of the best, through the power of that extravagant love, so that it does not come from the work, but it comes from the love.

The Israelites were and are the chosen people of God. It was to them that he made the first covenant. Israel was and always has been the "apple of His eye." He lavished them with love not because they were righteous, obedient and grateful but because He loved them. It wasn't a matter of him reciprocating the love that he felt towards them, He loved them although they squandered everything, he made for them, and cast it off like it was useless baubles, and trash. He loved them regardless of their love for Him. He loved them even though they rejected him. He will love them through all of eternity and his Holy heart will be broken when after all he has given them, they still chose the idols of stone and wood, rather than the living God.

Joel 1:14 – 15 KJVannotated

Sanctify ye a fast *(a call of God to his people: some translations say to consecrate, to set aside, this is a conscious decision of his people to respond to God's summons)*

call a solemn assembly – *(a solemn assembly, in other words, not a celebration, but a reconciliation)*

gather the elders and all the of inhabitants the of land *(this is a mandatory gathering, no one was exempted. A signification that God has something very important to say)*.

into the house of the Lord your God – *(a specific place for this gathering. Structure build exclusively for the worship of God*

and cry out to the Lord – *(the enter nation was of one accord, and cried out to God for their repentance,*

reconciliation, and restoration.)

Isaiah 58: 4- 7 annotated

Indeed, you fast for strife and debate, *(God explores the reason, motivation for their fasting)*

and to strike with the fist of wickedness. (what kind of a fast is this, that causes division and anger, this is not what I told you to do?)

You will not fast as you do this day, *(you have missed the point entirely, it isn't about you)* to make your voice heard on high. *(do you think that if you yell loud enough, I will hear you?)*

Is it a fast that I have chosen, a day for man to afflict his soul? *(this is how you fast as I have commanded you, do you suffer affliction for the soul of others in your fasting)*

Is it to bow down his head like a bulrush and to spread out sackcloth and ashes? *(this is symbolic of grieving, grieving over loss which can include the loss of a nation due to its sin and failure to respect God, and the mourning ceremonies which sometimes came with the fasting)*

Would you call this a fast and an acceptable day to the Lord? *(what do you think you are doing? This is a mockery).*

s Is this not the fast that I have chosen; *(this is what I have chosen, for you to be humble before me, and pray for those who need to be delivered from the oppression and the poverty)*

to loosen the bonds of wickedness, *(to continue to be a slave to iniquity and evil)*

to undo your burdens *(casting the burdens of your care and sin aside)*

to let the oppressed, go free *(to deliver and redeem from bondage)*

and that you break every yoke? *(freedom from adversaries and those who choose to harm)*

is it not to share your bread with the hungry and *(to share and not hoard for yourself)?*

that you bring to your house the poor who are cast out? *(hospitality that we are all called to do)*

When you **see the naked**, *(how can you see those without adequate clothing, ignore them, and still fast as I have requested)*

that **you cover him,** and *(physical needs must be met before the spiritual can)*

not hide yourself from your **own flesh.** *(neglect your own flesh and blood)*

Isaiah 58: 4-7 KJV

Indeed, you fast for strife and debate, and to strike with the fist of wickedness, you will not fast as you do this day, to make your voice heard on high. Is it a fast that I have chosen, a day for man to afflict his soul? Is it to bow down his head like a bulrush, and to spread out sackcloth and ashes? Would you call this a fast, and an acceptable day to the Lord? Is this not the fast I have chosen to loosen the bonds of wickedness, to undo the heavy burdens, to let the oppressed go free, and that you break every yoke? is it not to share your bread with the hungry, and that you bring to your house the poor who are cast out?

When you see the naked, that you cover him. And not hide yourself from your own flesh?

Rising again

The rose bloom red
The soft petals form
In the winter's dream
Long past the storm;
And when the spring
Bursts from the tomb
The blushing buds
Emerge from the tomb.

The touch of the hand
Pure and divine
Began the root
Before the start of time
And knew the thorns
It carries now
To be the ones
Forced upon his brow.

Blood crimson dripped
Upon his head.
All heaven knew
He would soon be dead
From wounds pierced
Through his holy skin
No one could tell
Of the love within.

Red rose, red rose
Blooming upon the bush,
Your velvet petals –
He made you first.
Beauty can only
Come from pain
And only Son shine
Can still the rain.

The words of Jesus John 2:18 KJV

"I tell you the truth. When you were young you were able to do as you liked; you dressed yourself and went wherever you wanted to go. But when you are old, you will stretch out your hands and others will dress you and take you where you don't want to go."

The hardest part of getting older, is when you realize because of your age you are not able to do a lot of the things you were used to doing in youth. Suddenly you discover that you can no longer stay up all night and be effective at work the next day. Handling the demands of your job becomes more difficult as each day passes. Additionally, you notice that it takes longer for you to recover from strenuous activity and illness. This can also affect you cognitively as your reflexes and thinking processes are not as quick and sharp as they used to be.

It is certainly difficult to face and accept the fact that you are getting older. Watching the aging of your parents can be quite traumatic to some. It was our parents, in most cases, that taught us essential things that we needed to know to navigate through life. They taught us about relationships, unconditional love,

and the family values inherit within the family. They gave us encouragement, lauds when we excelled, comfort when we did not. In the mind of a child, there is that concept that supposes they will be there forever, and that they can be counted on. They will be there always, in some capacity. It is an "always" connection regardless of the emotional aspect of family dynamics which can be challenging.

In a poem written by William Cowper we read that:

Peaceful hours I once enjoyed
How sweet their memory still,
But they have left and aching void
The world can never fill.

This implies that while other things can temporarily fill the void that your loved ones have left behind.

But the grieving never ceases, and the longing and the angst, like a never- ending thirst in the middle of the desert where there is nothing to quench it.

A further comparison would be with that of a blooming rose, vibrant, soft, a sense of comfort, amid fierce and destructive thorns. The possession of that exquisite is almost unattainable. One longs to reach for it, touch it, remove it from the thorny stem. However, there is a struggle to get to it. Its beauty and joy are attainable only at great risk, damage to life and limb, and perhaps even the possibility of death.

Jesus is the rose within the thorns. He created the eternal beauty of the rose, attractive to all with one narrow way of accessibility, that being through Him. He withstood the wicked thorns, despite heavy blood on his face when they were shoved upon his head. Amid desolation and untenable wilderness, he shows us that even in dire circumstances there is always hope. When he stood among those thorns, he longed to embrace us, to reach out to us in great suffering but could not because of the obstacles.

Knowing our own propensity to weakness and frailty, he chose to take the risk, so that we did not have to. He knew his fate; the incredible and horrific pain, crucifixion and the subsequent death. This rose, bruised and torn beyond recognition, still reached out to us. Because of the supreme sacrifice he bought for us a place where all grief, pain, tears and loss no longer exist. And there that rose will never fade.

Romans 8: 28-30 NKJV

And I am convinced that nothing can ever separate us from God's love. Neither death nor life; neither angels or demons, neither our fears for today nor our worries about tomorrow, not even the power of hell can separate us from God's love. No power in the sky above or the earth below – indeed, nothing in all creation can ever be able to separate us from the love of God that is revealed in Christ Jesus our Lord.

God's love

Faithless is he that says farewell when the road darkens.

J. R. R. Tolkien 1892 – 1973

Value far beyond any estimate
Can't be bought for any price
No one can ever possess it
Nothing other will suffice
No words can fair describe it.
Neither can it be contained
Yet all mankind desires it
And all are thus contained.

Many have never tasted it
Those who do can't get their fill
The thirst for it increases
For young, or old, or ill
And to those who are not afflicted
The joy of it prevails
Men have sought to keep it
And to the seven seas have sailed.

There are some who died in its defense,
Others shackled behind bars
There's no hope in human vessels
Or in alabaster jars.
Its fragrance is magnificent
And pales the scent of brilliant rose
Its softness so appealing
The roughest man seeks its repose.

In the shadows of the garden
Can be found it's sweet delight
It fades not in the sunshine
And hides not in the night
And while the world is sleeping

It does not stop or slow
Unchanging and unwavering
Beyond all that earth can know.

There is no spot where it is not
Be it ocean, sky, or hell.
Through the darkness of the night
The sin sick knows it well
It can't be contrived by humankind
Nor tame with command or rule
And those who try to discount it
Are anybody's fool.

What is this wonderful mystery
That wraps itself in words
And covers itself in blankets
Of everything true and good?
It cries passionately with agony
Yet rejoices with heightened joy
When one, once lost has found it
With the heart of a little boy.

Christ died that day to shed it
His blood for the people of earth
Though born in darkness they knew it
And became men of second birth.
Yet no human explanation
Can define this matchless love
From the sacred heart of Jesus
By His father's throne above.

The thing that gives me the greatest joy in my life is to write. Many things have come and gone, like people, horses and many other possessions or obsessions but one thing remains, to write. For some reason I feel the need to chronicle significant events, or things that made a great impression in my journals. Writing is something that I have done for a very long time. I become moody and frustrated when I have gone long periods without writing. Then when I finally engage in that activity the words fall onto the page like a waterfall sometimes too many for me to capture.

I'm always full of words and images. There is something every day that sparks a flame within me; always a moment when I have recognized the presence of God. There are simple things at first glance, but most are like icebergs. There is a small portion visible but a huge mountain beneath the surface. Unspoken, but hidden in the heart and soul of a person, these things are forever pondered. The expression can only disclose what it on the top missing the rest of the story.

God knows my "beneaths". He sees what we try to hide in darkness. The things "beneath," that we don't talk about are exactly what God sees in us. He knows the joy, but he also knows the angst, the grief, the anger, the disappointments, etc. He is within them. When my heart is broken so is His. He knows the feelings of loss, pain, abandonment; all the human realities. And He understands. He can see into the deep chambers of our soul. He comforts us by allowing us to have glimpses of the other side of darkness. This gives us hope and an incentive to hang on, rather than give up, when giving up seems to be the easiest to do.

In my opinion, the scripture passage 1 Corinthians 13 is the blueprint for love; loving one another, and loving God. Because there is so much beneath, we can't have full knowledge of the things of God within our earthly sphere. However, when we stand in front of the Throne of God, there will be no need for questions or guess. We will have the mind of Christ and nothing will be hidden from us. We will see the whole of the iceberg.

1 Corinthians 13 KJV, annotated

Tongues of men and of angels – limitation to communicate with those who speak different languages or from a different culture than our own. Paul speaks of the power of God in that not only does he know all languages, he has given us the ability to learn languages other than our own. He encourages us to do and say everything through the language of love. If we don't reflect the message of love, we are doing nothing but making loud noises.

And though I have the gift of prophecy …. and all knowledge, and the faith to use these gifts if I do not have an attitude of nurturing love, then it is all empty and useless.

What shall it profit you if words are spoken harshly to manipulate or control others with the coercion of fear?

Love never fails Eventually all things will fail but love endures forever.

Profits me nothing neither work, nor prayer, nor giving alms, nor help your neighbor, nor teaching others, if done without love, it is all ineffective and futile.

What does love do?   Love suffers long, (is very patient)
Love is always kind, (always even when you don't feel like it)
Love is not haughty, (being prideful or conceited)
Love does not boast, (unless your boast is in Christ)

Love is not rude, (interrupt, disregard, disrespect)

Love does not seek its own (trying to get things from others to satisfy self)

Love is not provoked (no matter how you are treated)

Love does not think of evil things (gossip, disparaging others, take advantage)

Love does not encourage iniquity, (enable, assist, agree)

Love bears all things, (he ain't heavy, he's my brother)

Love believes all things, (believing and living all things of God)

Love endures, (one does not get tired of loving)

All things "operated" by man, are not eternal, but things "operated" by God are forever.

When I was a child, I spoke as a child, (could only talk and understand childish things)

But when I became an adult, (a grown man or woman, I no longer had use for childish things and talk)

We are in a mirror for now (can only see and understand the reflections of our own world)

But then face to face (we will see our true selves as God intended for us to be)

Now we only know in part (we only have a small glimpse)

But then I will know and be known (no hidden things will remain)

And now abide faith, hope and love but the greatest of these are love (love is the foundation of all)

Though I speak with the tongues of men and of angels and have not charity (love) I am become as sounding brass, or a tinkling cymbal. And though I have the gift of prophecy and understand all mysteries, and all knowledge, and though I have all faith, so that I could move mountains and have not charity, I am nothing.

And though I bestow all my goods to feed the poor, and though I give my body to be burned, and have not charity, it profiteth me nothing.

Charity suffereth long, and is kind, charity envieth not; charity vaunteth not itself, is not puffed up. Doth not behave itself unseemly, seeketh not her own, is not easily provoked, thinketh no evil, rejoiceth not in iniquity, but rejoices in the truth; beareth all things, hopeth all things, endureth all things. Charity never faileth; but whether there be prophecies, they shall fail, whether there be tongues, they shall cease; whether there be knowledge, it shall vanish away. For we know in part, and we prophesy in part but that which is perfect is come, then that which is in part shall be done away. When I was a child, I spake as a child; but when I became a man, I put away childish things.

For now, we see through a glass darkly; but then face to face; now I know in part; but then shall I know even as I am known. And now abideth faith, hope and charity, these three, but the greatest of these is charity.

1 Corinthians 13 KJV

My God, empty me,
From all my
Presuppositions
And foregone conclusions.
Release me from the
Endless tyranny of
Expectation.
Banish from me
The ravages of regret
And erase from my mind
The disappointment from
False hope and dreams.
Remove from me the
Frustration of a plethora
Of broken promises
And the insidious pride
Of personal accolades.
Let me find joy in nothingness!
Teach me to seek only
To fill that vacant space with
The fulness and complexity
Of your extravagant love
And infinite presence.

I am a bad one to attempt to fill all the empty spaces in my soul with things that have temporary meaning. Attracted to colors, and drawing, and writing, and other stuff, I am prone to purchase things that I don't need just because they are unusual, attractive, or have a shiny package. When I am writing in my journal, I have developed the habit of using a different color each day that I write. The colors are not an indicator of any color-coding, or highlighting, or emphasizing. The colored pens that I use are sometimes gel pens, or just ball pens, sometimes a fountain pen. Later when I am leafing through the journal, I see pages of pink, blue, bright green, purple or whatever I felt like using that day.

There is a satisfaction I receive from choosing the color and the type of pen with which I write. I have discovered that I am a tactile person. I want to hold, feel, manipulate things in such a way that the movement of their usage have an impact on all my being, not just the scribblings on a page.

Sometimes I choose according to my present mood, or because a specific color reminded me of something. But sometimes it is just random, the first pen that I grab when I am preparing to write. The only time I have used the same color back to back has been when I am somewhere where my rainbow pens are not available.

The poems that you are reading within this book, are those that were birthed in my journals. After a bit of revision and editing they often can stand on their own, pointing to exactly the moment and the feeling of an experience or activity. Reading the entries and the poems that were sparked I am transported into that moment, and it is if as I am experiencing it all again. It keeps me connected to the parts of my past that are also a part of my present, and in some way, they are an indicator of what might be happening in my future.

I developed the habit of journal writing when I was in high school when we were required to record our thoughts, etc. in creative writing. Now it is just something that I do and when I don't have an opportunity to do so then it feels like my day has not started properly. I guess it is my way of talking to my environment, the universe and to God. Those journals are private, though I do sometimes share small portions, especially the poetry. The writing is written for no particular purpose except for the physical activity. It clears my mind, it sometimes solves my problems, and it functions as prayer to my God.

This is not the same world that I grew up it. The worldview has changed. People have changed. Things that were sacred are not special anymore. Communication is not done face-to-face over a lunch or a cup of coffee, but through texting, emailing, social media, and other electronic tools. Messages pop up on the screen of the device that is always with you, and that is where arrangements are made for meetups, stop-by visits, business communication and the like. People have become more individualized. One can walk through a shoulder to shoulder crowd, and without even looking at one another, a large percentage are mesmerized what they see on their phones. Pictures, selfies, messages, but not verbal communication.

And so, there is much that we lose as a society, as a people, as a resident on this planet. Relationships are superficial and fleeting. Families are fragmented, with members alienated from each other, going months, and sometimes years without seeing one another. Human posture is changing because of this phenomenon. We walk with heads down, backs bent, not looking at the ground, not looking at one another, but looking at what is on social media, or what is being texted. People have lost the ability to interact face-to-face. On occasion when one talks eye-to-eye to another it is usually an intense situation that cannot be handled electronically and is most likely negative.

Not only have we lost the ability to talk to one another, we have lost the ability to speak to God. Currently God does not use the facilities of social media, although he is perfectly able to do so. To talk to God requires the emptying of the noise of the world, and that which is of the mind. Seldom, do people put themselves in situations of silence, when the only thing they hear is the beating of their own heart. The stark quiet frightens those who are not used to it. Life loses its meaning, and it is easier to make foregone conclusions, or quick judgments on a single sound byte or maybe an image.

What would happen if for 5 minutes, the noise, the chaos, the confusion of the world, just stopped. No moving traffic, rushing subways, loud and annoying music, dog barking, or anything that would disturb the few moments of silence. One would be able, I am certain, to take a long and satisfying breath of air, instead of the stressful gasping that sometimes happens under stress, worrying or just the haste of navigating through the process of each day and through life. How would most people handle that? Would they think it is the apocalypse?

If we can fill the empty spaces within us, with the fulness and complexity, and the wonderfulness, of God's extravagant love, instead of with flashy things, noisy streets, and chaotic and disturbing notions and prideful expressions of self, then the world would be an entirely different place. It would in fact, be heaven. Sadly, when those brief moments of peace are revealed to us, we are clueless as to what to do with them.

If we concentrate on filling the vacant gaps within the deepest part of us, with something powerful, and eternal, then there would be no need for the disruptive and manic activity believed to be necessary to conquer anything in the scope of human experience. And every aspect of life would be meaningful to everyone.

Ecclesiastes 1:8 – 11 KJV annotated

All things are full of labor; (nothing is obtained that is obtained without effort)

man cannot utter it; (man cannot speak of the trials and the costs of these things which he wishes to obtain.

the eye is not satisfied with seeing, (one could see all the treasures of heaven and earth and still not be satisfied that there is not more).

nor the ear filled with hearing. (one could hear the greatest orator that ever existed or that will ever exist, and not be happy with the saying)

The thing that hath been, (what has already been established cannot be changed)

it is that which shall be; (it is what it is)

and that which is done is that which shall be done; (it is done, decreed, established, ordered, and unchangeable)

and there is no new thing under the sun (there is not one thing that has not been before)

is there anything whereof it may be said, See, this is new? (who can say that it has not happened before?)

hath been already of old time (we have seen this before; it is no different)

which was before us. (we weren't there, but our ancestors were, and so were the things we thought were new)

There is no remembrance of former things (what does it matter, no one will remember anyway)

neither shall there be any remembrance of things that are to come with those that shall come after. (and is there anyone who can say what is to come? All we know of is today, this moment)

Ecclesiastics 1: 8 - 11

All things are full of labor; man cannot utter it; the eye is not satisfied with seeing, nor the hear filled with hearing. The thing that hath been, it is that which shall be; and that which is done is that which shall be done; and there is no new thing under the sun. is there anything whereof it may be said, See, this is new? It hath been already of old time, which was before us. There is no remembrance of former things; neither shall there be any remembrance of things that are to come with those that come after.

The Thirst

Like a desert parched and dry, I thirsted with a depth unexplained.
I longed for the kiss of a breeze on my face and remembered the last time it rained.
In the heat of the day I carried the burden that grew heavy with each step I took.
But, true to the calling I kept pressing forward till I was so weary I shook.

My hunger, it drove me, I could not stay still, there was nothing that could satisfy.
Seeking safely His Presence and His Perfect will and the fountain that never runs dry.
I waited for no one, but searched for the place, the place where I knew He'd be found.
In the darkness I stumbled, groping for light. Surely, I'd find higher ground.

Then finally I got there, when it seemed all was lost. My body was battered and worn.
I had gone through hell, through the heat of the flame and I stood in the midst of the storm.
So thirsty I was that when I first saw Him, my throat was too dry to speak.
So hungry I craved one touch of His glory and I humbled myself at His feet.

Then He, without a word or a whisper sent His life-giving love to my soul.
He knew all the places that had been broken and by His command made them whole.
I, like the desert, when the rains finally came drank deeply till my thirst was quenched.

Washed by the Word, overcome by His Spirit, in His Presence I was fully refreshed.

Like a sponge I took in, reaching up to take more, and discovered an endless supply.
Like a river flowing under my feet, and the timeless expanse of the sky.
The joy of my heart leapt like a young calf, fighting to get free from its stall.
It had been a long time since I had come to the water, I had nearly lost sight of it all

"Come you that labor and are heavy laden here to the place of My rest.
You who are thirsty come drink from My River, you have passed the worst of the test.
Give me your burdens for my yoke is a small one and the weight that I give you is light.
You have cried out and when you felt hopeless, I heard you in the midst of the night.

Whether we know it or not we all have an innate hunger and thirst for the things of God. We are created in His image and he wants to abide within us. However, God being who He is gave us free will. He loved us so much that He gave us the ability to choose against Him. Why? Think of your children as an example. Mothers have told me that the love they had for their child far surpasses the love they have for anyone else. When children are born, they are immediately bonded to the one who bore them, carried them, planned for them and made a space in their home for them. I would venture to say that this bond, as a seed at birth, grows within the heart of mom and the heart of the baby. In this current world it appears that this bond is destroyed or at the very best ignored, and children both unborn, and
birthed are pushed away, and cast out as burdens that are too heavy, inconvenient and a disruption. However, what a joyous thing occurs when our offspring choose on their own to love and cherish those who gave them life.

As a human being created in God's image there is the same kind of a bond or connection. God's purpose in creating us is simply that He wanted to make us the object of His love. For the love to be reciprocal and genuine He gave us the opportunity to choose Him or reject Him. Otherwise we would be no more than puppets with no ability to express our feelings, to think on our own, and to move freely within our sphere of existence. This is a risky situation. How beautiful love is when it is unconditional, unprovoked, and genuine. It is a risky venture however because just as we can choose to love Him, we can also choose to reject him. He is willing to take that risk even though it breaks His heart. Even though He loves us whether we choose to love Him, or not, He will not force anyone into doing something they don't want to do and allows us to make our own decisions about who we choose to love, and who we don't.

He loved us first without waiting for reciprocation because it is His heart to do so. Oh, how He must weep when His children live as though He doesn't exist. We make things difficult for ourselves by choosing the hard way. We live according to our own desires and wants completely oblivious to the life we could have basking in the pure love of God. When you love someone, you want the very best for them. You want to shield them from hardship and adversity. You want to give them the world, which He has already done for us. If we don't accept the benefits of His love, then whatever is available for you is for naught. Like beautiful gifts beneath the Christmas tree, if they are not received and accepted, then all they are boxes with pretty paper stuck on them.

So back to the innate hunger and thirst that we have deep within our heart. What's up with that? Sometimes it takes a lifetime for people to recognize where that longing is coming from. Jesus is wooing us. He is calling us and wants to bestow all the benefits of His love to us. Think about this. The constant craving that is within you, will not go away with the acquisition of temporal things. It will not diminish when one reaches a certain stature or position. It cannot be quenched through wealth, nor in power. Yes, there may be temporary satisfactions when these things happen, but it is short-lived. It is not eternal.

Jesus desires for His children to flourish in Him. He wants us to cast all our desires and burdens on to Him. His back is strong enough to carry us through the worst parts of life, and He can rejoice with us when all is good. We may feel that we must give up everything that might give us pleasure, and sometimes what is important to us. But whatever worth or value that the world gives, is nothing next to the abundance that He wants to give to us. He not only wants to give us enough; He wants to give us unlimited love and riches according to His riches in Heaven. Why do we shortchange ourselves. His plan if for us to exchange our back-breaking and heart wrenching burdens, for the ones that He gives, which, if we are in Him, are not burdens at all.

Come: an open invitation. He is standing by the open door, waiting for you to enter.

unto me: to God and God alone, we will not find the rest for our souls until we rest in Him.

All you who labor to toil, to work, by the sweat of our brow, thorns and thistles, forever cultivating the land, the work, with no release from it until death.

And who are heavy laden; carrying our own loads and trying to carry the burdens of others. We are not to be burden bearers.

Take my yoke upon you; a yoke is a tool that is part of the harness for oxen, the most common working animal at that time. Most were designed for two oxen that had to be trained to work together

and to pull the weight at the same time so enough strength and power exerted together allowed the oxen to move forward with the burden.

learn from me; Jesus as the example, allowing the weight of the burden to fall on His back, so that the load for you is lighter and easier.

I am gentle: He is not the cruel taskmaster who would push the laborers far beyond their ability, and then violently punish them when they could not complete the task.

And lowly in heart: not haughty, demanding, ambitious, making himself as a ruler or dictator, but has no agenda, no requirements, and will not order others to do something that He would not do Himself.

and you will find rest for your souls. Not talking solely about physical rest here, but relief from the soul weary, and the dying of the spirit within. This is what He originally meant for us in the garden of Eden. This rest tells us that we are whole and full of the spiritual life again which we have been allowed to be depleted.

For my yoke is easy: not onerous or cumbersome but easy and does not require beyond what one can handle.

And my burden is light; not heavy and burdensome but is light and easy to carry because He carries it instead of you.

Matthew 11:28 – 30; Come to me all you who labor and are heavy laden, and I will give you rest. Take my yoke upon you, and learn from me, for I am gentle and lowly in heart and you will find rest for your souls. For my yoke is easy and my burden is light.

Job

The earthquakes shake
Unsettling earth's inhabitants
Turning walls into rubble
Uprooting trees from their roots
Nothing can stand

On the unstable ground;
Yet here I am to see the destruction.

the city gates lay under
the remains of walls
broken stones.
Pathways obliterated
No one goes in
No one goes out
And the remnants
Struggle to find sustenance
Beyond the barriers
That kept us safe and free.

Though my world has been
Pulled out from under my feet
And the sky's ugly storms assault me,
And no one remains to call my name
Though my clothes are torn
Leaving me half naked
Yet here I am in the ruins.
I will trust in the Lord.

What God gives can be taken;
Even if He sucks the life from me
Or buries me beneath the barriers and fences

Or remove my family from me
Of offers me no assistance
No relief from the deadening pain
That fully consumes me;
Even if my tears make oceans
And my mind screams from
The abyss of hell
And I exist no more
I will trust in the Lord

(written after hearing a sermon about the afflictions of Job)

And you think that your life is bad? Talk to Job. He lost everything and found that he had lost nothing.

There was not much more that could happen to him. In a timeframe of 24 hours, this man, a wealthy man, highly respected in the community, lost everything.

He was so confused and perplexed, and nothing made sense. This was truly human suffering; things far beyond his control. Job felt helpless to because there was nothing he could do. He felt hopeless because the suffering was so fierce and consuming. Would Job praise God in the middle of the chaos, or would he do, as his wife suggested, just curse God and die?

When we are suffering and in pain (be it emotional or physical), most are left with two choices. One can fight against the oppressor and hope that somehow, he could overcome or take flight away from the threat. At this point fear is what drives us to do either in most cases.

Job however did not seem to have these options. He was not physically strong enough to leave, and the threat was so huge that he could not stand against. His threat was the Almighty God. All Job could do was to sit upon the dung pile trying to cope with what had happened to him.

Job knew it was useless to try to argue with the Sovereign King of all. However, he was forced to engage in a lengthy debate with his friends who were determined to make understand that the reason he was in his current predicament was that he had done something sinful or offensive to God. Therefore, he needed to deeply search his soul to see what he had done to bring this all onto himself.

Job vehemently denied their accusation; hence the debate began.

Fast forward to our present time and situation. How often do we debate with God when we question what He is asking us to do? For some reason, we believe that God just doesn't understand our current situation. Surely, He knows the gravity of what He asks; doesn't He? Maybe He made a mistake and thought that He was talking to someone else. Why make me leave my self-constructed, comfortable and safe environment? Ultimately God always wins the argument.

Things were taken away from Job and he refused to despair. Instead, putting away his stature, his money, his possessions, family and finally his health, did not mourn. He may have been a bit humiliated when he sat on the dung heap but, even then he respected God's sovereignty. "in all this Job did not sin or charge God with wrongs." Job 1:22. Eventually he dialogues one on one with God and after a while all things was restored, God being his redeemer.

This was a session with God that allowed Job to be objective and plead his case. Job knew he was blameless in everything he did but was concerned that he inadvertently did something that he was not aware of. He, like, most of us believed that if he carried a contrite heart, God would shine favor on him, but if he had sinned, there would most certainly be destruction.

Job 38 complete chapter (annotated):

1 **Then the LORD answered Job** (Up until now, God was an eavesdropper in this conversation between Job and his three friends; here God speaks as the Almighty, the Prosecutor, the One with the ultimate authority).

out of the whirlwind, (God can choose to speak in the whirlwind and the storm, and, as he spoke to Elijah, He can speak in a small quiet voice) and said,

2 **Who is this** (that dares to speak)

that **darkeneth** (dares to speak)

counsel by words without knowledge? (as if he knows what he is talking about).

3 **Gird up now thy loins like a man**; (get serious now and stop being foolish, words used literally here).

for I will demand of thee and answer thou me. (now I will ask the questions and you will answer me).

4 **Where wast thou** (where were you?)

when I laid the foundations of the earth? (I set it so that it could not be moved).

declare, **if thou hast understanding** (if you know more than me).

5 **Who hath laid the measures thereof,**

if thou knowest? or who hath stretched the line upon it? 6 Whereupon are the foundations thereof fastened? or who laid the corner stone thereof; 7 When the morning stars sang together, and all the sons of God shouted for joy? 8 Or who shut up the sea with doors, when it brake forth, as if it had issued out of the womb? 9 When I made the cloud the garment thereof, and thick darkness a swaddling band for it, 10 And brake up for it my decreed place, and set bars and doors, 11 And said, Hitherto shalt thou come, but no further: and here shall thy proud waves be stayed? 12 Hast thou commanded the morning since thy days; and caused the dayspring to know his place; 13 That it might take hold of the ends of the earth, that the wicked might be shaken out of it? 14 It is turned as clay to the seal; and they stand as a garment. 15 And from the wicked their light is withholden, and the high arm shall be broken. 16 Hast thou entered into the springs of the sea? or hast thou walked in the search of the depth? 17 Have the gates of death been opened unto thee? or hast thou seen the doors of the shadow of death? 18 Hast thou perceived the breadth of the earth? declare if thou knowest it all. 19 Where is the way where light dwelleth? and as for darkness, where is the place thereof, 20 That thou shouldest take it to the bound thereof, and that thou shouldest know the paths to the house thereof? 21 Knowest thou it, because thou wast then born? or because the number of thy days is great? 22 Hast thou entered into the treasures of the snow? or hast thou seen the treasures of the hail, 23 Which I have reserved against the time of trouble, against the day of battle and war? 24 By what way is the light parted, which scattereth the east wind upon the earth? 25 Who hath divided a watercourse for the overflowing of waters, or a way for the lightning of thunder; 26 To cause it to rain on the earth, where no man is; on the wilderness, wherein there is no man; 27 To satisfy the desolate and waste ground; and to cause the bud of the tender herb to spring forth? 28 Hath the rain a father? or who hath begotten the drops of dew? 29 Out of whose womb came the ice? and the hoary frost of heaven, who hath gendered it? 30 The waters are hid as with a stone, and the face of the deep is frozen. 31 Canst thou bind the sweet influences of Pleiades, or loose the bands of Orion? 32 Canst thou bring forth Mazzaroth in his season? or canst thou guide Arcturus with his sons? 33 Knowest thou the ordinances of heaven? canst thou set the dominion thereof in the earth? 34 Canst thou lift up thy voice to the clouds, that abundance of waters may cover thee? 35 Canst thou send lightnings, that they may go, and say unto thee, here we are? 36 Who hath put wisdom in the inward parts? or who hath given understanding to the heart? 37 Who can number the clouds in wisdom? or who can stay the bottles of heaven, 38 When the dust groweth into hardness, and the clods cleave fast together? 39 Wilt thou hunt the prey for the lion? or fill the appetite of the young lions, 40 When they couch in their dens, and abide in the covert to lie in wait? 41 Who provideth for the raven his food? when his young ones cry unto God, they wander for lack of meat.

KJV

Aloneness
Makes for a long day.
No conversations
For distractions.
No flashing screens
Demanding acknowledgement
No loud voices or music
Just long hours of peace
And the sound of silence.

Once you speak it,
It has vanished.
It cannot exist
In a world of discord.
It has its own words
To communicate
In languages that
Only the soul understands.

Silence is pregnant
Always waiting
To give birth and
Release more than
Anyone can imagine.

It wells up like
A glorious fountain
Falling with abandonment
Down the side of the mountain
Spirit of silence
Please speak to me.
We were meant to dwell in
The beauty of silence.

Being alone is not the same as being lonely. Loneliness is normally that comes without choice, without pre-planning, in a state of isolation, and distress. Loneliness is the result of rejection, when one chooses not to accompany, join, or participate, or be in the presence of another. The one who is left alone, may fall into depression, and hopelessness, especially when they do not understand the reason for their perceived rejection. Often, it is magnified by anxiety, and the unfulfillment of expectations, on the part of the lonely person, perhaps without knowledge of the one that is the person who may cause the loneliness in the first place. Loneliness is a subjective thing as it may be driven by things that are hidden within the heart and mind of the one that is experiences it.

To be alone, however, which is what we are discussing here, indicates a mindful decision. Many people who consider themselves to be introverts, crave the times when they can be by themselves. These people are most usually writers, artists, musicians and those involved with any kind of creative art. It is in this atmosphere that the creativity is born. This allows the individual to work in a place that is quiet and free from distractions. As an introvert myself, I find this to be true. I cannot write or be creative when I am surrounded by noise and chaos, am constantly interrupted, and have no control over my environment. Given the opportunity to choose between a room full of people, or a quiet mountain retreat, I will most often choose the latter. This does not mean that I hate my fellow human beings but that I am uncomfortable if I am caught in a situation that is beyond my control.

I believe that Jesus was neither an extrovert, who pushed himself upon others, nor an introvert who shunned any interaction altogether. His heart was where the needs were, the sick, oppressed, dejected individuals that found no hope or encouragement from the company of their peers, or those they were required to serve. Jesus went where no one else would go; to the broken, the lost, the homeless, the discarded, and the poor.

However, even the most flamboyant extrovert needs time to recharge and to regather themselves. Stress is prevalent at the times when there is much activity, conflict, noise, excitement and so forth.

Prolonging stress can be detrimental to anyone who does not take the time to care for themselves and are always on demand for some reason or another. Mental and emotional breakdowns can occur when one is constantly confined by the demands of their position and responsibility. Many people are not able to take extended breaks or vacations for various reasons, and after a time, when they have realized no relief, their body begins to suffer from the pressure.

This is while Jesus made it a point to get off on His own, whenever He could, to recharge, and recover from the constant demands made upon Him. Yes, He is God, and within His divine nature, His power, strengths and resources were limitless. However, one must understand that when He lived on this earth, in human form, though He was still God, He became limited by the physical and human frailties that are present within all human beings. Therefore, He experienced hunger, fatigue, stress, loneliness, and anger. Those times alone were crucial for Him to maintain His connection with the spiritual facet of His relationship with His Father, the divine.

When Jesus was facing the crucifixion, He knew that He would be taxed beyond anything that could be imagined. The turmoil in the garden of Gethsemane was real, painful, and costly. Like anyone of us, who might be facing similar torture, He prayed to be spared from it. His prayers reflected the anguish that was a precursor to the agony that he faced. "Father," He prayed; "please remove this cup of suffering from me." Surely, he thought that there was another way to atone for the sinfulness of humankind but, he realized there was not. He could have made the decision to not partake of this horror.

He possessed the same free will that was granted to us. We are never forced to do anything, in most cases anyway, or be anything that we simply would prefer to avoid. We are not required to love, or give, or participate in the different elements of life. It is because of love that we feel constrained to give of ourselves to others, though sometime people will do "good deeds," because they receive a personal benefit from doing so.

So, what did Jesus benefit from making the decision to accept the Father's will for His fate? What does one receive to make such a sacrifice? To be willing to die for the sake of another does nothing for the one making such a decision. However, it releases another from the guilt and the punishment of that guilt and consequences. We are expected to love one another innately, to accept the differences of others, and to live as peaceably as we can with those that are in our sphere of interaction and influence. But, how many of us would be willing to lay down our life for the benefit of another.

Even though Jesus knew the seriousness and gravity of what He was asked to do, He was compelled by something stronger. Jesus was compelled, was driven by love. For us to receive redemption only one thing was possible. By His sacrifice, His suffering, His unspeakable pain, we received our atonement.

Taking part in aloneness then, gives us the opportunity to realize the magnitude of His love for us. There was nothing else He could do to express that love. The world was created to be an inhabitant for those whom He loved. God needed to express His extravagant love, so He created the object of His affection. We were uniquely made in His image. He gave us the ability to share in that love, to create, to choose, to enjoy and appreciate the beauty within one another and the world and universe that He made specifically for us. He did not make us as puppets because then we would not have the ability to choose Him and love Him and others freely. He gave us thinking minds with which we could understand and share His love with others. Forced love is not love at all but an automatic response innately implanted within to control us in some way. Chosen love is pure and genuine and joyous.

"For God so loved the world that He gave His only begotten Son, that whosoever believes in Him will not perish and have everlasting life."

John 6:15-21 KJV (annotated)

Therefore,

when Jesus perceived (He was attuned to their actions through the Holy Spirit, as it was not yet time for His sacrifice.

tha**t they were about to come** (they followed Him because of the miracles that He performed)

and take Him by force (this is not what Jesus wanted. He wants to sit on the throne in our hearts, not on some lavish throne in a palace. That will come later)

to make Him king (this was an attempt for the masses to control and contain Him, in which case He would not be able to reign freely, as this was a false kingdom, not the eternal Kingdom which will come later.)

He departed again to the mountain by Himself alone (all things were to be orchestrated by God alone, and therefore He needed to remove Himself from the intense emotions that they were displaying. This gave Him the opportunity to commune with His Father and do things according to His timing and sovereignty. In other words, God does not work according to the desires of humankind, but in and of the freedom of His own will and doing).

Now when evening came, (indicating that Jesus was apart from them for some time, was not hurried by human timetables or demands).

His disciples went down to the sea (no doubt that they went down to the sea expecting Jesus to be where they last left Him) got into the boat and went over the sea toward Capernaum. (it appeared that they were used to His practices. There are several occasions throughout the gospel that Jesus often separated Himself from His disciples for prayer and restoration.)

And it was already dark, and Jesus had not come to them. (perhaps there was a concern regarding the lateness of the hour, the developing of a storm, and not knowing where Jesus had gone)

Then the sea arose because a great wind was blowing. (because of the landscape surrounding the Sea of Galilee, a tunnel effect because of the surrounding mountains, it was easy for storms to developing quickly, without warning and becoming hazardous for those within boats away from the shore)

So, when they had rowed about three or four miles, (they were at the point of no return having been in the middle of the sea, their only option was to keep moving forward towards their destination)

they saw Jesus walking on the sea and drawing near the boat; (because of the stressfulness of the situation, with adrenalin at its highest they thought the worst when they saw an apparition approaching them)

and they were afraid. (there were seasoned fishermen on this boat. The storm must have been at an unusual intensity for them to be in so much fear)

But He said to them, (how they must have been comforted when they heard His voice)

"It is I, do not be afraid. (again, Jesus shows them His power and abilities and quickly comforts them)

then they willingly received Him into the boat, (alarm now relieved as their Savior is there for them)

and immediately the boat was at the land where they were going. (immediately they moved from the middle of the Sea of Galilee to Capernaum, their destination)

John 6:15-21 KJV

Therefore, when Jesus perceived that they were about to come and take Him by force to make Him king, He departed again to the mountain by Himself, alone. Now when evening came His disciples went down to the sea, got into the boat and went over the sea toward Capernaum. And it was already dark, and Jesus had not come to them. Then the sea arose because a great wind was blowing. So, when they had rowed about three or four miles, they saw Jesus walking on the sea and drawing near the boat; and they were afraid. But He said to them, "It is I; do not be afraid." Then they willingly received Him into the boat and immediately the boat was at the land where they were going.

In the depth of winter, I finally learned that within me lay an invincible summer.

Albert Camus 1913-1960

The western wall

And the schoolgirls stand before the western wall
Prayer books held gently in their hands
In one voice they look up and call
The creator of the land.

The prayers lift like incense
Burning in the censor
Girls rocking to the rhythm
Of a song that only they know.

Pure simple and genuine faces
Eyes bright to see it all.
"do you think He'll come today?"
"I don't know, we have to pray.

For less than a moment I touched it
As I stood in this holy place
I hoped God would accept my quiet homage
As I slipped my intentions into a crack.

The weathered stones welcomed
My prayers of faith
I have done all I can
The rest is up to Him.

When I visited Israel in 2018 my heart was opened to the land and its people, God's chosen. I, a gentile (grafted in because of the compassion of Christ) born in the United States cannot fully understand what it is like to be born in the Holy Land. Israel is one of the smallest countries on the planet, but her legacy belongs to the world.

I write this at the season of Rosh Hashanah, the beginning of the Jewish new year and the annual time of atonement. In 2019 this celebration began on the evening of Sunday September 29 and ended on the evening of Tuesday October 1. Rosh Hashanah (may also be called the Feast of Trumpets) is a commemoration of thankfulness. This is done by praying in the temple, personal prayer and reflection, and the hearing of the shofar and making burnt offerings to God. In the Biblical Hebrew this holiday is called Yom Teruah – which means literally "days of shouting or blasting." There is also the time of Yom Kippur which signifies the end of the last ten days of penitence that are part of the Rosh Hashanah holiday.

In the book of Leviticus 23:23 – 32 it is written that this Feasts of trumpets (et al) was established during the time of Moses when God's law was implemented. This observance begins with a Sabbath rest, a proclamation marked by the blowing of trumpets, or more traditionally the Shofar which is made from a ram's horn, burnt offerings and a convocation that includes the reading of the law. No regular work was done at this time and those at the convocation meet with the same heart and mind. This is considered the most significant of the Jewish holidays and feasts.

The tenth day of that same month was set aside as the day of atonement. On this day burnt offerings were done and were profound because of what they symbolized. Prior to the sacrifice, all the utensils and articles used were sanctified. In addition, each person was required to go through a searching of the soul so that all they could seek penitence for all the wrongdoings they committed during the previous year.

These observances were designed to bring God's people together to remember that they were indeed his Chosen Ones. While they were wandering in the wilderness, God instructed them to build memorial altars to mark significant events. He wanted them to have a way of remembering who they were and whose they were. In Israel there are many places that have been designed as eternal memorials such as the remaining stone walls of the old city of Jerusalem. The western wall specifically is also known as the wailing wall. This wall serves as a spiritual contact with the living God of Israel. People from all over the earth, come to this wall to pour out their hearts to Him.

It is customary for these pilgrims to write out their petitions on small slips of paper. These prayers then are pushed into the crevices and cracks on the wall. In this action of devotion many of them will touch and kiss this sacred wall. Once a month the pieces of paper are removed and buried on the Mount of Olives. Sometimes young school students will pray at this wall. Gathered in small groups they will recite their prayers from their Hebrew prayer books, as the anticipate the coming of their Messiah.

Leviticus 25: 23-32 NKJV

Then the **Lord spoke to Moses** saying; (the Lord spoke to Moses as a friend in the tent of meeting).

"**speak** to the children of Israel saying, (Moses then functions as the messenger and the mediator between God and His people)

"in the **seventh month, on the first day of the month**, (Heshvan, on the Jewish calendar, considered to be the Jewish New Year because it is believed to correspond with the 7th day of creation, the day that God created Adam and Eve. Note of interest: this year 2019 is year 5780 on the Jewish calendar)

you shall have a **sabbath-rest**, (a period of time set to commune with God, and partake in worship, "rest" indicates that no work be done on that day).

a **memorial blowing of the trumpets**, (the blowing of the trumpets heralded the arrival of the seventh month and the beginning of the Days of Awe between the feast of trumpets and the Day of Atonement during which time the people repent of their transgressions in preparation.)

a **holy convocation** (a gathering of all the people to commemorate the event, listen to the reading of the law, and worship God).

You shall do no **customary work** on it (daily work will stop, and all work pertaining to the sabbath celebration are done prior to sunset).

And you shall offer an **offering made by fire to** the Lord. (burnt offerings, sacrifices required of God from his people for specific reasons, most importantly, atonement, typology for the permanent sacrifice made by Jesus the Son of God in the Gospels.)

And the Lord spoke to Moses saying;" the tenth day of this month shall be the **Day of Atonement** (an everlasting statute for you, to make atonement for the children, for all their sins, once a year. God is holy and it was His desire that we should remain holy as he is holy. However, because He gave us the gift of free choice and will, we squandered that gift choosing to go our own way rather than that which he had set out for us. Was to be done on a specific day in a specific month for perpetuity.)

You shall afflict your souls (examine your heart, is it intently evil? What is within the heart that is contrary to God's command to us. Preparation for aforementioned offerings remains the same).

For it is the Day of Atonement **to make atonement for you** before the Lord. (demonstration of His love for us, even though we are burdened with sin, anything that is put in place before God, even own personal offenses, He still provided a way to be redeemed)

For every person **who is not afflicted in soul** (he or she that disregards and chooses to not take responsibility for wrongdoings)

That **same person shall be cut off** from his people. (the one who continually chooses to go against the rules, or the commands of God, and is blatantly making such choice, cannot participate in the things of God until repentance occurs. Basis for excommunication in the church.)

And **any person who does any work** (as one above who disregards the directive, should be considered as one who blatantly makes a choice of disobedience)

Shall be destroyed from his people (not only is this person shunned, because of his/her choice to keep the day Holy as God commanded, can no longer live in community.

You shall do **no matter of work** (God is clear. Only those which priestly functions are responsible for the sacrificial requirements)

It shall be a **statute forever** throughout your generations and all your dwellings. (a statute that was set for perpetuity.)

It shall be to you a **sabbath of solemn rest.** (In this sense it is just not engaging in common work, it is also an engagement of the mind and soul as to why this sabbath is taking place, to worship, reflect on, contemplate God)

And **you shall afflict your souls** on the ninth day of the month (again another reckoning, a command to reflect on how one lives and how one interacts with others, and with God – again to be done on a specific day, from evening to evening)

You **shall celebrate** your Sabbath (not to be seen as an onerous activity but as a day to connect with God and with family without outside distractions)

Leviticus 25: 23-32 NKJV

Then the Lord spoke to Moses saying;" speak to the children of Israel saying, "in the seventh month, on the first day of the month, you shall have a sabbath-rest, a memorial blowing of the trumpets, a holy convocation. You shall do no customary work on it; and you shall offer an offering made by fire to the Lord."

And the Lord spoke to Moses, saying; "also the tenth day of this month shall be the Day of Atonement. It shall be a holy convocation for you, you shall afflict your souls, and offer an offering made by fire to the Lord. And you shall do no work on that same day, for it is the Day of Atonement to make atonement for you before the Lord. For every person who is not afflicted in soul on the same day, that same person be cut off from his people. And any person who does any work on that same day, that person I will destroy from among his people. You shall do no matter of work; it shall be a statute forever throughout your generations and all your dwellings. It shall be to you a sabbath of solemn rest, and you shall afflict your souls on the ninth day of the month, at evening, from evening to evening, you shall celebrate your Sabbath.

Dreams are made of glass.
That's why they end up broken
Like books were never written
And words were never spoken
Ground into tiny fragments
Or held within a hand.

Why am I so persistent
To think that I have a chance
When dreams are so illusive
One can't risk a look askance.

In a breath or an eye blink
It is as if it were never there
And the place from whence it came
The heart – has lost its care.

Perhaps, I have expected too much from my life. Perhaps, I should not have expended so much effort seeking dreams that were impossible to realize. I didn't have much direction in my youth and believed that if I wanted something bad enough, and long enough, and was willing to work hard enough, eventually my dream would manifest itself. Back then, dreams were just a reality that I had not yet experienced.

I believed in Santa Claus long after other children gave up on the idea. Somehow, the things on my list appeared beneath the Christmas tree year after year. I was amazed that I could get what I wanted by just asking for it (except that I didn't get the pony, but that's another story). I am not saying that I would get just one or two things from my list, but practically everything I had carefully written in my elementary school handwriting. Along with the things that I had asked for, there were also surprises; stuffed animals, clothes for my dress-up dolls, clothing, and always books.

Something happens to the heart of a person when one discovers that Santa, the Easter Bunny, Tooth fairies and the like were only make-believe. The magic disappeared, along with the brightness of the celebration, especially that of Christmas. Suddenly, it felt like the hope had been diminished, and there was little to look forward to. Now, the coming of the advertised "most wonderful time of the year," becomes more a season of stress and anxiety. In fact, there is an underlying feeling of dread and the unspoken wish that it would just hurry up and go away.

This is a hard confession for a Christian to make. Isn't Christmas supposed to be the time of year when hope is the brightest and joy is prevalent wherever you go? Aren't there supposed to be the singing of carols and the expectations of miracles? What about the pureness of the newly fallen snow and the gathering of snow angels on the front lawn? To me it seems that the Christmases of my youth set false expectations that have been a permanent disappointment in my adult years.

How bleak was that first Christmas as an adult, that I was on my own, and alone, and struggling to figure out my life? The joy of giving was not something I was going to partake in, because I lived broke, paycheck, to paycheck, to paycheck. If I had $20 left in my bank account, the day before the next payday I felt like I had accomplished something. I could not buy gifts for others. I did attempt to make things to give as gifts but unfortunately my resolve disintegrated before the holiday was in full swing. This was the first, of many years that followed, that changed my perception of Christmas and covered it forever under a dark cloud.

Such are dreams. Dreams are like shining stars that pierce the darkness of night. Dreams are the hope of a new morning, or the promise of spring on the coldest day of winter. To have lost the heart of a dream is like having it be "always winter but never Christmas," as the children discovered when Narnia was still in the grip of the white witch. How much easier it is to dismiss a dream rather than risk the disappointment that prevails when it can't be realized. Wrapping oneself up in the burden of work becomes a great way to avoid participation in meaningless frivolity and emptiness. Participating in such activities becomes little more than obligations. Unfortunately, sometimes such obligations lead us into places of vulnerability that we would prefer not to face.

The word "validation," is one that is always in the back of my mind. According to the GOOGLE dictionary, there are a couple of definitions to consider. The first is a need of a person to believe that one's opinions or feelings are valid and worthwhile. Most have exaggerated necessity for acceptance and validation. Synonyms include; confirmation, documentation, proof, evidence, testament and substantiation.

Writing for me is a venue for what dreams I have left. It is the main dream that still gives me a measure of hope. I am not sure if the amount of effort I put into the activity will produce anything of value but throughout the years I have discovered that the suppression of this causes great frustration and grief. I have swept up the shattered dreams of my life more than one. Pieces, like that of broken glass, swept into the dustpan and tossed into the trash. I have seen the sparkle in the fragments turn into dust and each word lose its reason. I have seen all the horses that I have ever ridden, ever owned, run ahead of me leaving me behind in a pile of hay. I have prayed that God would remove the burden of that dream from me because I could no longer manage it. All I have left from that is a beat-up old saddle, a pair of riding boots, and a photo of me on horseback. But it was necessary for me to let it go.

And it's true – when a dream is lost, the heart stops caring for it, stops longing for it and assumes that it is fruitless to continue to pursue. It is like a little bit of death occurs, there is now a void that remains as does the memory of a dream that no longer exists. Throughout the years that realization that dreams die, or are lost, or just ultimately rejects becomes a common and expected outcome. Soon it seems that more dreams are lost than are realized and one gets used to the new activity of learning to let it go.

The Lord Jesus Christ loves us and longs for us to have the desire of our hearts. However, it takes some work before we discover that the truest desire, the truest yearning is for Him. I see that it becomes easy, and still does, to attempt to fill those empty places within us, with things, people, activity, possessions, that provide us with temporary gratification and fulfillment. How often does one exert an extreme amount of effort investing in something only to find out in the end that it isn't enough, that there is still hunger for more, new, and different.

Bruce Springsteen sings that *"everyone has a hungry heart,"* though he doesn't define the object and the depth of that hunger. No truer words were even sung or spoken. St Augustine of Hippo says, *"You have made us for yourself, O Lord, and our hearts are restless until they rest in you."* Are they not both saying the say thing? The difference is that the former speaks of the hunger inherent in all of us, while the latter speaks of its satiation. For us to reach out to our Lord brings our deepest desire to fruition. Our heart becomes entwined with His making us one with our Beloved. He is the fulfillment of every desire and every thirst we could ever have. Our dreams maybe made with breakable, inflexible glass that looks shiny and lovely on the surface but break into horrid little pieces of pain and disappointment. His dreams are fluid and alive, and while they are unchanging, they flex and move within us by the unction of His Holy Spirit that becomes the Fountain which is eternal.

Various scriptures annotated and full text:

Job 17:11 KJV My days are past (**my best days are over**).

My purposes are broken off (**what of my plans? The things I wanted to do?**)

Even the thoughts of my heart (**my desires, my dreams, those things that I hoped for, and worked for**).

Job 17:11 KJV-- My days are past. My purposes are broken off, even the thoughts of my heart.

Psalm 20:4 KJV May He (**He the Lord God Almighty**)

Grant you (**give to you freely**)

Your heart's desire (**those things which you have longed for and dreamed of**)

And fulfill (**complete, finish, bring to fruition**)

All (all of them, not just one, or two but every single one)

Your purpose (to what you were created and designed to do with meaning and with joy)

Psalm 20:4 KJV– May He grant you your heart's desire and fulfill all your purpose.

Psalm 21:2

You (stated directly to God)

Have given him (God's child, follower, the one who desires God).

And have not withheld (holding nothing back, no restrictions, no restraints, no limitations)

The request of (the seeking, asking, praying, etc.)

His lips (out of the heart does a person speak, deeper than mere understanding, is assimilated and becomes part of …)

Psalm 21:2 KJV– you have given him his heart's desire and have not withheld the request of his lips. Selah.

Psalm 73:25 KJV

Whom have I? (who else can I rely on? Where is the solid rock on which to stand? Who can I trust?)

In heaven (who is on my side that can see the whole distance?)

None upon earth (none "other")

I desire (the longing and the dreaming)

Besides You **(who can compare with you?)**

Psalm 73:25 KJV – whom have I in heaven but you? And there is none upon the earth that I desire besides you.

Psalm 103:5 KJV

Satisfies your mouth **(you fill up my senses)**

With good things **(taste and see that the Lord is good)**

Your youth **(not physical youth but a reawakening of the hopes, dreams and desires for the future)**

Like the eagles **(so that you can soar again without encumbrance)**

Psalm 103:5 KJV– who satisfies your mouth with good things, so your youth is renewed like the eagles.

Psalm 132:13 KJV

For the Lord **(God almighty, who is, who was and who is to come)**

Has chosen **(God chose Zion specifically to be His dwelling place – as He has chosen the heart of the individual for the same purpose)**

He has desired it **(wanted it, admired it, longed for it, created it for His purpose)**

As His dwelling place **(to abide, to inhabit, to dwell)**

Psalm 132:13 KJV– For the Lord has chosen Zion; He has desired it for His dwelling place.

Psalm 145:15 KJV

The eyes of all (**every person seeks after Him**)

Expecting a response (**expecting a response even if they don't realize who or what they are seeking**)

And You give them food (**spiritual food, physical food, all of what they need**)

In season (**not necessarily when they request, but rather at the time it is the most needed for His glory**)

Psalm 145:15 KJV– the eyes of all look expectantly to You, and You give them food in season.

Proverbs 10:24 KJV

The fear of the wicked (**those who are wicked constantly fear retribution and consequences for their transgressions. Added note: In a conversation with one who is wicked it might be very difficult to see the fear within them because they have become expert in hiding it, but it is manifested in everything they do, and every decision they make.**)

The desire of the righteous (**those who are righteous according to God's law and will, will desire good things and because they are living with the desire to love and please God, will be rewarded**).

Proverbs 10:24 KJV– the fear of the wicked will come upon him and the desire of the righteous will be granted.

Proverbs 11:23KJV

The desire of the righteous (**becomes transformed by God's desire for them and is therefore good**).

The expectation of the wicked is wrath (**because all they desire is what they can selfishly and foolishly gain but remain angry because it does not fulfill the eternal longing of their soul**).

Proverbs 11:23 KJV – the desire of the righteous is only good but the expectation of the wicked is wrath.

SOS 7:10 KJV

I am (**who I am, what he has desired me to be**)

His desire is towards me (**He delights in me and therefore I desire him**)

SOS 7:10 KJV – I am my beloved's and his desire is towards me.

Hosea 6:6 KJV

Mercy and not sacrifice (**sacrifice being only a superficial attempt at atonement, but mercy can only be received through surrender**)

Knowledge of God (**more than just knowing about Him. It is knowing Him intimately as one would know a beloved spouse**).

Hosea 6:6 KJV – For I desire mercy and not sacrifice and the knowledge of God more than burnt offerings.

My blue veined hands
Writes in my own blood
Letting the words drip
On to the page.

The noise of my soul
Screams in my own voice
As the sound rises like incense
To no one.

I am all by myself
Though many voices saturate
Through the silence --
No one speaking.

Sealed away
As if in a womb
Hands reaching out
Finding nothing to touch.

His nail-pierced hands
Writes my name upon
The hollow of His palms
Teaching me life.

Grace, the handhold that
Raises me from the darkness
Into His glorious
And incredible light.

The stains of His blood
Engraves the sacrifice
Of His extravagant love
Into my stony heart.

For some time now I have been fascinated by the hands of others (and sometimes my own) because I see them as fine working tools, that can lift heavy objects or perform precision and minute tasks. The hands of those who work in construction, moving heavy objects, or manipulating equipment that can move such objects shows, that it isn't a matter of just moving items from one place to another but also having the ability to determine exact placement and adjustment, measurement, and location of the object being placed. Conversely, think of the surgeon who has the skill to use his or her hands to make incisions, corrections, replacements or just repair on the human (or in the case of a veterinarian, animal) body.

There are those who use their hands to communicate, such as those who employ sign language to speak to others who cannot hear, or hand signals, used in the course of sporting and other types of events, or to use electronic devices for digital communication. Then there are the compassionate caregiving hands, which with one helps another in ways that he/she can no longer do for themselves, or for the very young which have not yet learned what hands are for.

Enjoy the guitarist, or violinist, pianist, and others who have mastered the art of music; or the artist who renders paintings, sculptures and other types of art, or the writer, who with the stroke of a key on the computer, or the movement of a pen, creates stories, and poetry, and research documents, books, etc. Fingers to run through the hair, or to massage an aching back, or to stroke the soft fur of a cat, or to hold a telescope with which to see the universe beyond; To cook, then to eat, then to touch. The list can be developed into thousands of pages and still not be exhaustive.

As I write this, I am drawn to the memory of S who, when I knew her was in middle school and high school. I was assigned to the job of transporting her to school, and sometimes to other things. In the beginning of this work I was a bit apprehensive as I had never encountered someone with such severe disabilities. She was bright, eager to learn, and loved being around others. Going to school was not a drudgery for her, as it enabled her to interact with friends, co-students, and others. I was nervous because I didn't want to do anything wrong, hurt her in any way, offend her, or draw unneeded attention to her. For me, as one who was already prone to be self-conscious and depressed, I would often project myself into the situations of others, and with my own emotions and imagination, try to envision how they lived.

After a time, because of S's enthusiasm about, and her determination to do all that others told her that she could not, I didn't see her as handicapped anymore. I no longer noticed that she had been born without arms or legs, because it didn't hamper her in anyway, and she was often more active than those who I knew that had no physical limitations. As I got to know her, I saw her excel in art, particularly, drawing and painting, in singing, and in academics. It sometimes made me ashamed of myself in that I believed that there were many things I didn't have the ability to do. I was hard on myself often because I wasn't the athlete I wanted to be, or the artist, or the beauty pageant queen, struggling always to be who I wasn't. This inner struggle was so prevalent within me that a lot of the time, instead of engaging in life, in activities, in relationships, I hung back, worried about not being able to do something right the first time I did it, or not being able to speak properly in front of groups, and certain people, or not believing that I was smart enough to get the same good grades as did my peers.

It was so different with S. Her viewpoint on life and living was remarkable. The very things that others told her that she would never do, were the exact things that she pursued. Going to a ceramic class with her mother and I she quickly out did me as she painted the ceramic figure that she worked on. Each shape and line she painted was as straight and as perfect as that of a professional, with no mistakes, or "going beyond the lines," or the mixing of colors. There were no errant paint drizzles on the table, no overfilled and globby brushes, no do overs and no unsightly messes to clean-up. Using a paint brush held firmly in her month she was able to write, and draw, and paint in ways that I would not have dreamed of being able to myself. Was she upset about the missing limbs? If she was, she did not display any negative emotions. What she did is to improvise by doing the best she could by what she had to work with.

Now, there was much behind the scenes that I didn't see. I did not see the frustration that she might have experienced when those on whom she depended let her down. I did not see the sadness in her face that might have occurred when she realized that something that she really wanted to do was not possible for her. I did not see any worry that she might have voiced when others here age were actively dating and gathering with friends. I did not see her apologize for her existence. I did not see her withdraw from things because she felt useless and worthless. I am not saying that this all didn't happen. But I know that with me, when I am desiring to do something and find that I cannot for some reason, I would become frustrated, depressed, withdrawn, and hopeless.

I have heard people say that," you don't miss what you never had." For a long time, I didn't quite understand what was meant when that was said. I focused on the unfairness of it all. It, in my viewpoint, wasn't fair that my best friend could draw wonderful things, and I could barely make a circle; or that she had a mother that was very active in creative things, costumes, household decorations, art, music, etc., while it seemed that my own mother's soul purpose in life was to clean the house. when I saw others that were successful in just about everything they did, sports, grades, people skills, art, I wondered where I had been when all the talents were passed out.

I learned enough to get by, so that it would look on the surface of things that I was handling things fine, accomplishing enough, and somewhat happy with my life to not draw too much scrutiny. But I always knew that I would always exist in the average zone, not failing much but also not exceling either. For me work was hard, even with the simplest things and I am not sure if it was because I was simply too hard on myself, or I just had a lower level of capability than everyone else. I could make others believe that I was educated and skilled but deep in the darkest part of me, I knew I was not.

Talking about hands, is more than a discussion regarding the appendages at the ends of your arms. While beautiful in nature with a plethora of working parts, sinewy bands of connection, muscles that give strength, and bones, joints and cartilage that provide movement, there is so much more. Hands are useless unless connected to the heart. The heart, the mystical center of the human being drives the hands into motion. From this heart comes the nuances of thought, personality, emotionality, physicality and spirituality. This indicates how we respond to the world that we live in and how we accept our own circumstances and situations.

The activity of the hand reflects the condition of the soul, the deepest part of a person. using a hand to violently harm another does nothing but allows others to see the evil that lurks inside. Using hands to create shows the wonder that happens when one is attached to the creative attribute of out creative God. King David writes about the preparation of his hands to do battle in the defense of God's people. Jesus heals with a mere touch of His divine hand. Moses raises his hands to part the Red Sea so that the people of Israel can pass through.

There could be times when the follower of Christ grows tired in well doing, or just from the vagaries of life. Do we not have the tendency to pull back our hands when the light of our heart grows dim? Do we not become reluctant to expend ourselves when the things of God are unclear to us? Do our hands become worn and callused from toil and heavy labor? Our hands are the reflection of our soul. How do we handle the presence of God? How do we execute His will upon this earth? What do we give to others? What do we selfishly keep for ourselves?

NOTES

NOTES

NOTES

NOTES

NOTES

NOTES

NOTES

NOTES

NOTES

NOTES

Printed in the United States
By Bookmasters